100 True Soliloquies
for Women

Smith and Kraus *Books for Actors*

MONOLOGUE AUDITION SERIES

The Best Men's / Women's Stage Monologues of 2000
The Best Men's / Women's Stage Monologues of 1999
The Best Men's / Women's Stage Monologues of 1998
The Best Men's / Women's Stage Monologues of 1997
The Best Men's / Women's Stage Monologues of 1996
The Best Men's / Women's Stage Monologues of 1995
The Best Men's / Women's Stage Monologues of 1994
The Best Men's / Women's Stage Monologues of 1993
The Best Men's / Women's Stage Monologues of 1992
The Best Men's / Women's Stage Monologues of 1991
The Best Men's / Women's Stage Monologues of 1990
One Hundred Men's / Women's Stage Monologues from the 1980s
2 Minutes and Under: Character Monologues for Actors Volumes I and II
Monologues from Contemporary Literature: Volume I
Monologues from Classic Plays 468 BC to 1960 AD
100 Great Monologues from the Renaissance Theatre
100 Great Monologues from the Neo-Classical Theatre
100 Great Monologues from the 19th Century Romantic and Realistic Theatres
The Ultimate Audition Series Volume I: 222 Monologues, 2 Minutes & Under
The Ultimate Audition Series Volume II: 222 Monologues, 2 Minutes & Under
    from Literature

YOUNG ACTOR MONOLOGUE SERIES

Cool Characters for Kids: 71 One-Minute Monologues
Great Scenes and Monologues for Children, Volumes I and II
Great Monologues for Young Actors, Volumes I and II
Short Scenes and Monologues for Middle School Actors
Multicultural Monologues for Young Actors
The Ultimate Audition Series for Middle School Actors Vol.I: 111 One-Minute
    Monologues
The Ultimate Audition Series for Teens Vol. I: 111 One-Minute Monologues
The Ultimate Audition Series for Teens Vol.II: 111 One-Minute Monologues
The Ultimate Audition Series for Teens Vol.III: 111 One-Minute Monologues
The Ultimate Audition Series for Teens Vol.IV: 111 One-Minute Monologues
The Ultimate Audition Series for Teens Vol.V: 111 One-Minute Monologues
    from Shakespeare
Wild and Wacky Characters for Kids: 60 One-Minute Monologues

If you require prepublication information about upcoming Smith and Kraus books, you may receive our semiannual catalogue, free of charge, by sending your name and address to *Smith and Kraus Catalogue, PO Box 127, Lyme, NH 03768. Or call us at (800) 895-4331; fax (603) 643-6431.*

100 True Soliloquies
for Women

edited by Jennie Wyckoff

MONOLOGUE AUDITION SERIES

A SMITH AND KRAUS BOOK

Published by Smith and Kraus, Inc.
177 Lyme Road, Hanover, NH 03755
www.SmithKraus.com

First Edition: November 2003
10 9 8 7 6 5 4 3 2 1

Cover illustration by Lisa Goldfinger
Cover design by Julia Hill Gignoux

Library of Congress Cataloging-in-Publication Data
100 true soliloquies for women / edited by Jennie Wyckoff. —1st ed.
p. cm. — (Monologue audition series, ISSN 1067-134X)
Companion vol. to: 100 true soliloquies for men.
ISBN 1-57525-303-8
1. Monologues. 2. Acting—Auditions. I. Title: One hundred true soliloquies for women.
II. Wyckoff, Jennie. III. 100 true soliloquies for men. IV. Series.
PN 2080.A16 2003
808.82'45—dc22
2003061469

NOTE: These monologues are intended to be used for audition and class study; permission is not required to use the material for those purposes. However, if there is a paid performance of any of the monologues included in this book, please refer to the permissions acknowledgment pages 130–136 to locate the source that can grant permission for public performance.

Contents

AGNES OF GOD

John Pielmeier

Doctor Martha Livingstone, 40s – 50s
1979, Canada

The Doctor, addressing the audience, gives us a brief history of her relationship with the Catholic church.

DOCTOR. Oh, we would get into terrible arguments, my mother and I. Once, when I was twelve or thirteen, I told her that God was a moronic fairy tale — I think I'd spent an entire night putting those words together — and she said, "How dare you talk that way to me," as if *she* were the slandered party. And shortly after Marie died, I became engaged for a very short time to a very romantic Frenchman whom my mother despised, and whom consequently I adored. We screamed ourselves hoarse many a night over that man. (*She laughs.*) And you know, I haven't thought of him in years. I haven't seen him since I left him — no, *pardonnez-moi*, Maurice, since *he* left me. What finally happened was that I . . . well, I . . . I was pregnant and I didn't exactly see myself as a . . . well, as my mother. Maurice *did*, so . . . (*Silence.*) And then once, in Mama's last years when she was not altogether lucid, I told her in a burst of anger that God was dead, and do you know what she did? She got down on her knees and prayed for His soul. God love her. I wish we atheists had a set of words that meant as much as those three do. Oh, I was never a devout Catholic — my doubts about the faith began when I was six — but when Marie died I walked away from religion as fast as my mind would take me. Mama never forgave me. And I never forgave the Church. But I learned to live with my anger, forget it even . . . until *she* walked into my office, and every time I saw her after that first lovely moment, I became more and more . . . entranced. (*Silence.*) Marie. Marie.

AGNES OF GOD

John Pielmeier

Doctor Martha Livingstone, 40s – 50s
1979, Canada

In this passage we hear the Doctor's dilemma with Agnes.

DOCTOR. A psychiatrist and a nun died and went to heaven. At the pearly gates, Saint Peter asked them to fill out an application, which they did. Upon looking at their papers, he said, "I see you both were born on the same day in the same year." "Yes," said the doctor. "And that you have the same parents." "Yes," said the nun. "And so you're sisters." The nun smiled knowingly but it was the doctor who answered, "Yes." "And you must be twins," said the saint. "Oh, no," the two of them said, "we're not twins." "Same birthday, same parents, sisters, but not twins?" "Yes," they answered, and smiled. I found this riddle, casually and coincidentally, on page thirty-three of an ancient issue of a defunct magazine. By this time, I was convinced that Agnes was completely innocent. I had begun to believe that someone else had murdered her child. Who that person was, and how I was to prove it, were riddles of my *own* making that I alone could solve. But the only answer I could come up with was upside down on page 117. (*Silence.*) They were two of a set of triplets. My problem was twofold: I wanted to free Agnes — legally prove her innocence — and I wanted to make her well.

AGNES OF GOD
John Pielmeier

Doctor Martha Livingstone, 40s – 50s
1979, Canada

Here, the Doctor reflects on the tragedy of Agnes.

DOCTOR. (*Singing.*) "Yes, he gets his girl some candy." I don't know the truth behind that song. Yes, perhaps it was a song of seduction, and the father was . . . a field hand. Or perhaps the song was simply a re-membered lullaby sung many years before. And the father was . . . hope, and love, and desire, and a belief in miracles. (*Silence.*) I never saw them again. The following day I removed myself from the case. Mother Miriam threw Agnes on the mercy of the court, and she was sent to a hospital . . . where she stopped singing . . . and eating . . . and where she died. Why? Why was a child molested, and a baby killed, and a mind destroyed? Was it to the simple end that not two hours ago this doubting, menstruating, non-smoking psychiatrist made her confession? What kind of God can permit such a wonder one as her to come trampling through this well-ordered existence?! I want a reason! I *want* to believe that she was . . . blessed! And I *do* miss her. And I hope that she has left something, some little part of herself, with *me*. That would be miracle enough. (*Silence.*) Wouldn't it?

AGNES OF GOD

John Pielmeier

Doctor Martha Livingstone, 40s – 50s
1979, Canada

Addressing the audience, the Doctor gives us her reasons for helping Agnes.

DOCTOR. I remember when I was a child I went to see Garbo's *Camille,*
oh, at least five or six times. And each time I sincerely believed she would
not die of consumption. I sat in the theater breathless with expectation
and hope, and each time I was disappointed, and each time I promised
to return, in search of a happy ending. Because I believed in the existence
of an alternate last reel. Locked away in some forgotten vault in Hollywood, Greta Garbo survives consumption, oncoming trains, and firing
squads. Every time. I still want to believe in alternate reels. I still want
to believe that somewhere, somehow, there is a happy ending for *every*
story. It all depends on how thoroughly you look for it. And how deeply
you need it. (*Silence.*) The baby was discovered in a wastepaper basket
with the umbilical cord knotted around its neck. The mother was found
unconscious by the door to her room, suffering from excessive loss of
blood. She was indicted for manslaughter and brought to trial. Her case
was assigned to me, Doctor Martha Livingstone, as court psychiatrist, to
determine whether she was legally sane. I wanted to help . . . (this young
woman, believe me.)

AGNES OF GOD

John Pielmeier

Doctor Martha Livingstone, 40s – 50s
1979, Canada

The Doctor comes to a touching realization in this moment.

DOCTOR. I dreamt that night that I was a midwife in a small private hospital in a faraway land. I was dressed in white and the room I was in was white, and a window was open and I could see mountains of snow all around. Below me on a table lay a woman prepared for a cesarean. She began to scream and I knew I had to cut the baby out as quickly as possible. I slipped a knife into her belly, then reached to my wrists inside. Suddenly I felt a tiny hand grab hold of my finger and begin to pull, and the woman's hands pressed down on my head, and the little creature inside drew me in, to the elbows, to the shoulders, to the chin, but when I opened my mouth to scream — I woke up, to find my sheets spotted. With blood. *My* blood. My rather sporadic menstrual cycle had ceased altogether some three years before, but on that night it began again. *(Silence.)* What would I have done with a child? Nothing. Nothing. *(Silence.)* The next day I asked for and received an order from the court allowing Agnes to return to my care. You see, I was so sure I was right. As a doctor, perhaps, I should have known better, but as a person — *(She begins to beat her chest with her fist.)* I am not made of granite. I am made of flesh and blood . . . and heart . . . and soul . . . *(She continues viciously to beat her chest in silence for a few moments, then stops.)* This is it. The unfinished thought. The last reel. No alternate in sight.

ALL'S WELL THAT ENDS WELL

William Shakespeare

Helena, 20s – 30s

Determined, Helena speaks to the audience.

HELENA. Our remedies oft in ourselves do lie,
      Which we ascribe to heaven; the fated sky
      Gives us free scope; only doth backward pull
      Our slow designs when we ourselves are dull.
      What power is it which mounts my love so high,
      That makes me see, and cannot feed mine eye?
      The mightiest space in fortune nature brings
      To join like likes, and kiss like native things.
      Impossible be strange attempts to those
      That weigh their pains in sense, and do suppose
      What hath been cannot be. Who ever strove
      To show her merit that did miss her love?
      The king's disease — my project may deceive me,
      But my intents are fix'd, and will not leave me.

ALL'S WELL THAT ENDS WELL

William Shakespeare

Helena, 20s – 30s

Here, Helena speaks about Rossillion.

HELENA. "Till I have no wife I have nothing in France."
      Nothing in France until he has no wife!
      Thou shalt have none, Rossillion, none in France;
      Then hast thou all again. Poor lord, is't I
      That chase thee from thy country, and expose
      Those tender limbs of thine to the event
      Of the none-sparing war? And is it I
      That drive thee from the sportive court, where thou
      Wast shot at with fair eyes, to be the mark
      Of smoky muskets? O you leaden messengers,
      That ride upon the violent speed of fire,
      Fly with false aim; move the still-piecing air
      That sings with piercing; do not touch my lord.
      Whoever shoots at him, I set him there;
      Whoever charges on his forward breast,
      I am the caitiff that do hold him to't;
      And though I kill him not, I am the cause
      His death was so effected. Better 'twere
      I met the raving lion when he roar'd
      With sharp constraint of hunger; better 'twere
      That all the miseries which nature owes
      Were mine at once. No; come thou home, Rossillion,
      Whence honour but of danger wins a scar,
      As oft it loses all; I will be gone;
      My being here it is that holds thee hence.
      Shall I stay here to do't? No, no, although
      The air of paradise did fan the house

And angels offic'd all. I will be gone,
That pitiful rumour may report my flight
To consolate thine ear. Come, night; end, day;
For with the dark, poor thief, I'll steal away.

ANDROMACHE

Jean Racine, Translated by Richard Wilbur

Hermione, 20s
1660s, Greece

Hermione tells us about her dilemma.

HERMIONE. Where am I? What have I done? What must I do?
What clouds my heart? What cleaves my brain in two?
All through this palace, aimlessly I move.
Alas, I know not whether I hate or love.
Oh, with what cruel eyes he took his leave! —
No pity in them, no pretense to grieve.
Was there a moment's pain or mercy shown?
Could I extract from him a single groan?
Dumb to my sighs, unmoved by my dismay,
Did he seem touched by me in any way?
And I still pity him! Worse yet, my heart
Is cowardly enough to take his part!
I tremble at his danger, and though my will
Cries out for vengeance, I forgive him still!
No, I'll not cancel what my anger swore:
Let the man perish! He lives for me no more.
The traitor mocks my stormy rage, and sneers,
Thinking that it will dissipate in tears;
That, weak and wavering, I'll interpose
One arm to shield him from the other's blows.
He fancies that I'll be, as ever, kind.
But no, the wretch has other things in mind:
Triumphant in the temple, he does not give
A thought to whether I'd have him die or live.
The villain leaves that bitter choice to me.
Well, let Orestes act, let Pyrrhus be
Destroyed; he knew to what his treason led,

And forced me, in the end, to wish him dead.
To wish him . . . what? Have I ordered such a thing?
Because I've loved him, must he die? This king
Whose exploits it was my delight of old
To hear again, and yet again, retold,
To whom my secret heart was given, in fact,
Long, long before our ill-starred wedding pact —
Can I have come so far, traversing all
These seas and countries, only to plot his fall,
To slay him, murder him? Oh, lest they kill him now —

ANNE OF THE THOUSAND DAYS

Maxwell Anderson

Anne, 20s
1536, England

Anne talks about her impending execution.

ANNE. I've never thought what it was like to die.
    To become meat that rots. The food for shrubs,
    and the long roots of vines.
    The grape could reach me.
    I may make him drunk before many years.
    Some one told me the story
    of the homely daughter of Sir Thomas More,
    climbing at night up the trestles of London Bridge
    where they'd stuck her father's head on a spike,
    and hunting among the stinking and bloody heads,
    of criminals, still she found her father's head,
    his beard matted and hard with blood.
    And climbing down with it, and taking it home.
    To bury in the garden, perhaps.
    Would they fix me head up on London Bridge?
    No. Even Henry would object to that.
    I've been his queen. He's kissed my lips.
    He wouldn't want it. I'll lie in lead — or brass.
        Meat. Dead meat.
    But if my head were on the Bridge he wouldn't climb
        to take it down.
    Nobody'd climb for me. I could stay and face up the
        river,
    and my long hair blow out and tangle round
    the spikes — and my small neck.
    Till the sea birds took me,

and there was nothing but a wisp of hair
and a cup of bone.
I must think of something to say when the time comes.
If I could say it — with the axe edge toward me,
Could I do it? Could I lay my head down —
and smile, and speak? Till the blow comes?
They say it's subtle. It doesn't hurt. There's no time.
No time. That's the end of time.

ANNE OF THE THOUSAND DAYS

Maxwell Anderson

Anne, 20s
1536, England

Anne reflects on her relationship with Henry.

ANNE. If I were to die now —
　　but I must not die yet,
　　not yet.
　　It's been too brief. A few weeks and days.
　　How many days, I wonder, since the first time
　　I gave myself, to that last day when he —
　　when he left me at the lists and I saw him no more?
　　Well, I can reckon it.
　　I have time enough. Those who sit in the Tower
　　don't lack for time.

　　He could never cipher.
　　He was shrewd and heavy —
　　and cunning with his tongue, and wary in intrigue,
　　but when it came to adding up an account
　　he filled it with errors and bit his tongue —
　　and swore —
　　till I slapped his hands like a child and took the pen
　　and made it straight.
　　"A king," I said, "a king, and cannot reckon."
　　I was his clever girl then, his Nan;
　　he'd kiss me then, and maul me, and take me down.
　　On the rushes. Anywhere.
　　Why do I think of it now? Would he kill me? Kill me?
　　Henry? The fool? That great fool kill me?

Could I kill him, I wonder?
I feel it in my hands perhaps I could.
So — perhaps he could kill me. —
Perhaps he could kill me.

If I die now, I go out into night,
and Elizabeth, my firstling, all I have,
must face the new world in the morning.
To those who die we seem to go forward into darkness.
To those who are new-born we seem to go forward into dawn.
As I bore Elizabeth, midnight will bear morning.

AS BEES IN HONEY DROWN

Douglas Carter Beane

Ginny, 20s
1990, New York

Ginny, a young violinist walks on timidly. Topless, she is covering her breasts with her crossed arms.

GINNY. Mr. Uhm . . . Mr. Morelli. Please don't cry. I'm sorry. I just — It's my mom, she's not what you would call, in any meaning of the word, worldly and she — she wouldn't understand me getting my picture taken without my shirt clutching myself with a vacant yet sensual look on my face. And what it has to do with my violin recitals. But if you think it's what I should do to — please stop crying — if you think it's what I should do to get some recognition and — take my picture. I have my shirt off. You can take my picture. See?

AS YOU LIKE IT
William Shakespeare

Rosalind, 20s – 30s

Alone, Rosalind speaks the Epilogue.

ROSALIND. It is not the fashion to see the lady the epilogue; but it is no more unhandsome than to see the lord the prologue. If it be true that good wine needs no bush, 'tis true that a good play needs no epilogue. Yet to good wine they do use good bushes; and good plays prove the better by the help of good epilogues. What a case am I in then, that am neither a good epilogue, nor cannot insinuate with you in the behalf of a good play? I am not furnished like a beggar, therefore to beg will not become me. My way is to conjure you, and I'll begin with the women. I charge you, O women, for the love you bear to men, to like as much of this play as please you. And I charge you, O men, for the love you bear to women — as I perceive by your simpering none of you hates them — that between you and the women the play may please. If I were a woman, I would kiss as many of you as had beards that pleased me, complexions that liked me, and breaths that I defied not. And I am sure, as many as have good beards, or good faces, or sweet breaths, will for my kind offer, when I make curtsy, bid me farewell.

THE BEAUTY QUEEN OF LEENANE

Martin McDonagh

Maureen, 40s – 50s
Present, Ireland

Maureen fills in the blanks.

MAUREEN. To Boston. To Boston I'll be going. Isn't that where them two were from, the Kennedys, or was that somewhere else, now? Robert Kennedy I did prefer over Jack Kennedy. He seemed to be nicer to women. Although I haven't read up on it. *(Pause.)* Boston. It does have a nice ring to it. Better than England it'll be, I'm sure. Although where wouldn't be better than England? No shite I'll be cleaning there, anyways, and no names called, and Pato'll be there to have a say-so anyways if there was names to be called, but I'm sure there won't be. The Yanks do love the Irish. *(Pause.)* Almost begged me, Pato did. Almost on his hands and knees, he was, near enough crying. At the station I caught him, not five minutes to spare, thanks to you. Thanks to your oul interfering. But too late too late to be interfering you are now. Oh aye. Be far too late, although you did give it a good go, I'll say that for you. Another five minutes and you'd have had it. Poor you. Poor selfish oul bitch, oul you. *(Pause.)* Kiss the face off me, he did, when he saw me there. Them blue eyes of his. Them muscles. Them arms wrapping me. 'Why did you not answer me letter?' And all for coming over and giving you a good kick he was when I told him, but 'Ah no,' I said, 'isn't she just a feeble-minded oul feck, not worth dirtying your boots on?' I was defending you there. *(Pause.)* 'You will come to Boston with me so, me love, when you get up the money.' 'I will, Pato. Be it married or be it living in sin, what do I care? What do I care if tongues'd be wagging? Tongues have wagged about me before, let them wag again. Let them never stop wagging, so long as I'm with you, Pato, what do I care about tongues? So long as it's you and me, and the warmth of us cuddled up, and the skins of us asleep, is all I ever really wanted anyway.' *(Pause.)* 'Except we do still have a problem, what to do with your oul mam, there,' he said. 'Would an oul folks home be too harsh?' 'It wouldn't be too harsh but it would be too expensive.' 'What about your sisters so?' 'Me sisters wouldn't have the bitch. Not even a half-day at Christmas to be with her can them two stand. They clear forgot her birthday this year as well as that. 'How do you stick her without going off your rocker?' they do say to me. Behind her back, like. *(Pause.)* 'I'll leave it up to yourself so,' Pato says. He was on the train be this time, we was kissing out the window, like they do in films. 'I'll leave it up to yourself so, whatever you decide. If it takes a month, let it take a month. And if it's finally you decide you can't bear to be parted from her and have to stay behind, well, I can't say I would like it, but I'd understand. But if even a year it has to take for you to decide, it is a year I will be waiting, and won't be minding the wait.' 'It won't be a year it is you'll be waiting, Pato', I called out then, the train was pulling away. 'It won't be a year nor yet nearly a year. It won't be a week!' *(The rocking chair has stopped its motions. Mag starts to slowly lean forward at the waist until she finally topples over and falls heavily to the floor, dead. A red chunk of skull hangs from a string of skin at the side of her head. Maureen looks down at her, somewhat bored, taps her on the side with the toe of her shoe, then steps onto her back and stands there in thoughtful contemplation.)* 'Twas over the stile she did trip. Aye. And down the hill she did fall. Aye. *(Pause.)* Aye.

THE BEGGAR'S OPERA

John Gay

Polly, 20s
1700s, England

Not knowing what to do, Polly speaks to us.

POLLY. Now I'm a wretch, indeed — methinks I see him already in the cart, sweeter and more lovely than the nosegay in his hand! — I hear the crowd extolling his resolution and intrepidity! — What volleys of sighs are sent from the windows of Holborn, that so comely a youth should be brought to disgrace! — I see him at the tree! The whole circle are in tears! — even butchers weep! — Jack Ketch himself hesitates to perform his duty, and would be glad to lose his fee, by a reprieve. What then will become of Polly? As yet I may inform him of their design, and aid him in his escape. It shall be so. But then he flies, absents himself, and I bar myself from his dear, dear conversation! That too will distract me. If he keep out of the way, my papa and mama may in time relent, and we may be happy. If he stays, he is hanged, and then he is lost forever! He intended to lie concealed in my room, till the dusk of the evening. If they are abroad, I'll this instant let him out, lest some accident should prevent him.

BLUES FOR MISTER CHARLIE

James Baldwin

Jo, 50s – 60s
1960s, Mississippi

Jo passes out coffee to while speaking to invisible guests.

JO. Am I going to spend the rest of my life serving coffee to strangers in church basements? Am I? — Yes! Reverend Phelps was truly noble! As *usual!* — Reverend Phelps has been married for more than twenty years. Don't let those thoughts into your citadel! You just remember that the mind is a citadel and you can keep out all troubling thoughts! — My! Mrs. Evans! You are certainly a sight for sore eyes! I don't know how you manage to look so unruffled and *cool* and *young!* With all those *children.* And Mr. Evans. How are you tonight? — She has a baby just about every year. I don't know how she stands it. Mr. Evans don't look like that kind of man. You sure can't tell a book by it's cover. Lord! I wish I was in my own home and these were *my* guests and my husband was somewhere in the room. I'm getting old! Old! Old maid! *Maid!* — Oh! Mr. Arpino! You taken time out from your engineering to come visit here with us? It sure is a pleasure to have you! — My! He is big! and dark! Like a Greek! Or a Spaniard! Some people say he might have a touch of nigger blood. I don't believe that. He's just — *foreign.* That's all. He needs a hair cut. I wonder if he's got hair like that all *over* his body? Remember that your mind is a citadel. A citadel. Oh, Lord, I'm tired of serving coffee in church basements! I want, I want — Why, good evening, Ellis! And Mr. Lyle Britten! We sure don't see either of *you* very often! Why, Mr. Britten! You know you don't mean that! You come over here just to see little old *me?* Why, you just go right ahead and drink that coffee, I do believe you need to be sobered up!

CATHOLIC SCHOOL GIRLS

Casey Kurtti

Maria Theresa, 13
1960s, New York State

Here, we hear about Maria Theresa's dream life.

MARIA THERESA. Late at night when I'm lying in my bed, I ask my-self some math questions and I get all the answers right. Then when I wake up and go to school and all the way there and all the way through religion class and on the line to go to the lavatory, the answers are still in my head. But just right before math class, they have fallen out of my brain when I wasn't thinking to hold them in. I am not stupid, even though my parents and Sister think so. If we had math first thing, maybe they wouldn't go away. Sometimes, if my father comes home from work early, he helps me with my math homework. I don't want him to because if I give the wrong answer he gets mad and hits me. Usually my mother makes him stop but sometimes she is giving one of the babies a bath and she doesn't hear me. I think about math almost every single night. I can't help it. It makes me feel weird so I usually make a plan for a good happy dream so that when I do fall asleep I won't have a scary one. My favorite dream right now is that I live with someone else's family. Like I live with Donna Reed and I am the only child except that I have an older brother and sister. Donna Reed sends me to a school where there is no math or spelling. When I come home from school, my older brother takes me for a ride to the candy store in his yellow convertible. I make him put the top down and I sit in the back and my older sister combs my hair gently for a whole hour and lets me play with her make-up. Then we all get dressed up for dinner and we go downstairs. Donna Reed always cooks something real good for dinner. Stuff like steak or turkey with mashed potatoes and gravy. She never makes eggplant parmesan and tuna casse-role. Dessert is always on the table so right after you finish your dinner you can just grab your dessert and eat it. Usually it is My-T-Fine choco-late pudding because Donna Reed knows that is my favorite. After the family is finished we are excused from the table and we go into the living room and everyone gathers around while I play the piano. Then my father, Mr. Reed, picks me up and carries me up the stairs to my room and tucks me into my very own canopy bed. He puts my stuffed animals around the bed so I will be safe and he leaves my Raggedy Ann and Andy night-light on so I won't be scared. Donna Reed kisses me on the forehead and tells me what a wonderful and beautiful daughter I am and how glad she is that she adopted me and I fall asleep. Sometimes I pray to Jesus about something. Jesus tells me not to think that my parents don't love me. He says that they will probably not get mad at me if I bring home another bad mark in math and spelling. So I believe him, but something always happens when I get home anyway.

CATHOLIC SCHOOL GIRLS

Casey Kurtti

Colleen, 13
1960s, New York State

Colleen tells us about becoming a woman.

COLLEEN. I used to go out with this guy, Ricky. I liked him a lot for
awhile. We hung around Cross County Shopping Center on Saturdays.
We used to get red pistachio nuts and then we'd wait till our hands got
all red and sweaty. Then we'd go upstairs on the escalator to the Wedding Shop and smear all the white dresses with our hands. It looked like
The Bride of Frankenstein, I swear. One time we went to the movies on
a Friday night. Me and Ricky saw *Born Free.* It was okay for awhile but
then toward the end it got bad. The girl lion gets killed and it's really sad.
I started to cry even, but I didn't let that Ricky see. I hate to let a boy see
me cry. The day we broke up, Ricky and me were sitting in the back of
his father's car in the garage. He gave me his ID bracelet and then he tried
to put his hand somewhere. I ran right out of that car but I kept the
bracelet just for spite. I told my mother about it. Me and my mother are
just like this. (*Holds two fingers together.*) She told me I did the right thing.
Then she started giving me a speech about sex stuff. She told me about
the change and how it was part of becoming a woman. She told me when
I got it, it would be such a happy day that we would go out to lunch and
have a party all day long. Just me and her. Ha. I don't want to be a woman.
I like myself the way I am. My chest is growing, and I think there is hair
coming out of, you know, down there. Well anyway, Sister told everyone
to finish up with their desks and to pack up. I felt something. I tried to
close my legs so it would stop. I held my stomach in, real hard, but it
kept leaking. I didn't know the whole thing was so messy. I didn't want
to move. I took my sweater off and wrapped it around me. I knew what
it was. After Monica put the wastebasket back, Sister Mary Germaine told
me to take my seat. But even before I started to move, she asked me about
my sweater. She thought I was trying to show off with sex or something,

I guess. She said, "Take that sweater off, it's seventy degrees in this classroom." "My stomach hurts, it makes me feel better." "I'll ask you one more time, take it off." The boys began to come into the classroom, she didn't care, she let them. I couldn't look at her. She hit me. I put my hands to my face and she ripped the sweater off, digging her nails into my side. I just stood there against the blackboard. Everyone was looking at me. Then she made an announcement to the class, that in all her years of teaching, she had never come across someone with such a lack of concern for their personal hygiene. She said these things right in front of the boys. I thought I was going to die. A couple of drops of blood got on the floor. She made one of the boys go down to the janitor's closet and get a mop. The nurse came in and took me out of class. I never want to go back there again. She is trying to make me feel guilty. I do feel guilty. I am a jerk. I wish I was dead, and never had to see you or anybody else again. I wish I had never become a woman. I'm no good at it. Is that what you wanted to hear, Sister? All right, I'm no good at it.

CATHOLIC SCHOOL GIRLS

Casey Kurtii

Elizabeth, 13
1960s, New York State

Elizabeth tells off God.

ELIZABETH. (*To God, as if she is in church.*) Hey, come on out, I want to talk to you. It's me, Elizabeth. You can hide behind any statue in this place, but you better listen to me. I don't know if you know this but after my grandmother moved in with us, everything was different. We used to sit in my room, after school. She'd ask me questions about all sorts of things. Then she'd listen to my answers real close because she said I was an important person. Some nights, after we went to bed, I would hear her talking to my grandfather in the dark. If I made any noise she'd stop. Because it was private. One night I saw that she was crying. I made some noise and she stopped. Then she asked me if I remembered my grandfather. I did, she liked that. We fell asleep on her bed like sisters. Sunday mornings were kind of strange. Nobody would give up eating bacon and some smells made her sick. My father would tell her if the grease bothered her so much, to take her eggs and go into the bedroom and wait until breakfast was over. I helped her stuff towels into the cracks under the door; but the smell got in anyway. Then my father would make me come back to the table and eat with the rest of the family. I'd go, but I wouldn't eat that bacon. Sometimes, if she was feeling a little better we'd take short walks. After we had rested, she'd tell me stories about my mother and bring along pictures that I had never seen. I didn't know why my mother was so sad and neither did my grandmother. One day, my father came home from work and told me that my grandmother would have to move back to the Bronx. He said it was just not working out. She needed more care and besides she was making the family crazy. I told him that she wasn't making me crazy. I told him she let me be near her. He didn't understand that. And now I see that you didn't either. You took her I don't think that's fair. You're supposed to do the right thing, all the time. I don't

25

believe that anymore. You just like to punish people, you like to interrupt their lives. You didn't let me finish. She doesn't know what I think, and I was almost ready to tell her. Why don't you take my mother next time? Oh, you like to take little kids, don't you? Grab one of my brothers next, they're all baptized. Why don't you take my whole stinking family, in one shot, then you won't waste any time. That would be some joke. But I want to tell you something. It's a personal message, I'm delivering it, myself. Don't you ever lay your hands on me, cause if I ever see you, you can strike me dead . . . try . . . I will spit all over your face, whatever it looks like. Because you and everyone else in this world are one big pack of liars. And I really think I hate you. Something else: You don't exist.

CATHOLIC SCHOOL GIRLS

Casey Kurtti

Wanda, 13
1960s, New York State

Wanda tells us about her dreams of fame.

WANDA. My father comes home from work every night and before he even takes off his gray hat with the skinny feather, he drops a bag of leaky, smelly meat on the table for my mother. She waits to see if she should kiss him or not. If it is just hamburger, she grunts. If it is liver, she practically goes to Mars. I hate liver. I hate all things sometimes. Even things I like. My ballet lessons, my pedal pushers, my dolls on the shelf, and I hate my smartness. You know why, because they were given to me. I am working on something that's mine. I have been for a long time. After school I go home and do my homework right away so I can go down to my father's store. He's not really a bad man, I just don't like him or something. While he is in the back room, sawing those bones out of the big legs of meat, I take soda cans and crush them onto my shoes. I move some sawdust into a little pile on the floor and I begin to dance. Not like Nancy Sinatra or Diana — oh, I am so much better. As I'm dancing, my mind just lets go and all these little movies come into my head. My favorite — I'm on the Ed Sullivan Show. (*Mimes being handed a microphone.*) Thank you, Eddie. I'm singing a song. Fake snow is falling all around me. I have on a sexy dress. It's sort of a sad song and I look so incredibly beautiful, that some people in the audience are starting to cry. Well, I break into a tap dance just to cheer them up. Later on Ed Sullivan brings me back stage to the Beatle's dressing room and Paul asks me to marry him. I say, maybe in a couple of months, because I have my career to think about. I become an international superstar and I go live in a penthouse apartment right on top of Radio City Music Hall. (*Starts to put on go-go boots.*) So for now I don't mind rehearsing in my father's store. He stays out of my way. I don't care if my hands and feet stick out a little too much, that can be fixed. I don't mind being Nancy Sinatra, I like these go-go boots a lot anyway. I made my mother buy them for me at S. Klien's. So here is DAWN GABOR, who used to be Wanda Sluska, coming to you live, right after eighth grade, to sing and dance, just because she feels like it. So you just get those TV sets warmed up, because even if it is a sin, I don't care, I'm going to be famous. Wait. Watch for me. Okay?

COLLECTED STORIES

Donald Margulies

Lisa, 20s – 30s
1990s, New York City

Lisa nervously stands at a lectern and speaks into a microphone to the assembly.

LISA. Hello. (*She clears her throat, sips water.*) Hi. Thank you so *much* for that. It's so nice to be here at the 92nd street Y, and be a part of this long literary tradition. I'm really honored. Thank you. I never expected such a turnout. Wow. I'm Lisa Morrison, by the way — just in case you're in the wrong room. (*A beat.*) Um . . . (*Takes a deep breath.*) I'm a little nervous. Forgive me. I'm new at this. I've never spoken in front of so many people before. I guess as long as I speak clearly, and with conviction, this should go reasonably well. It's important that you're able to *hear* me. At least that's what I was taught, and I was taught by a master. (*She scans the audience looking for Ruth, but doesn't see her. She takes a sip of water, then a deep breath.*) What I'd like to do, for starters, I'd like to begin with an extract from my new novel — what am I talking about?, my *first* novel, my *only* novel — *Miriam's Book*, which is being published next month by Viking? (*Corrects herself.*) By Viking. And then, if my voice holds up — (*Clears her throat for effect.*) — I thought I'd read one or two stories from my debut collection from a couple of years ago, *Eating Between Meals.* (*There is scattered applause, which surprises and amuses her.*) Gee. Well! I feel like Joni Mitchell in *con*cert all of a sudden. (*Imitating a fan.*) "Do 'Circle Game'!" (*A beat.*) Anyway, rather than describing too much about the book, I thought I would just start at the beginning. How's that? (*A beat.*) *Miriam's Book.* (*A beat.*) The prologue is titled "Night Falls Fast," which is taken from a poem called "Not So Far As the Forest" by Edna St. Vincent Millay that appears in the beginning. Do you know that poem?, are you familiar with it? (*A beat.*) Shall I read it ? Okay, why don't I. (*A beat. Deep breath.*) "Not So Far As the Forest"

THE COUNTRY WIFE

William Wycherley

Mrs. Pinchwife, 30s – 40s
1600s, England

Mrs. Pinchwife can't decide what to do.

MRS. PINCHWIFE. 'For Master Horner' — So, I am glad he has told me his name. Dear Master Horner! But why should I send thee such a letter that will vex thee and make thee angry with me? — Well, I will not send it. — Ay, but then my husband will kill me — for I see plainly, he won't let me love Master Horner — but what care I for my husband? — I won't, so I won't send poor Master Horner such a letter — but then my husband — But oh, what if I writ at bottom, my husband made me write it? — Ay, but then my husband would see't — Can one have no shift? Ah, a London woman would have had a hundred presently. Stay — what if I should write a letter, and wrap it up like this, and write upon't too? Ay, but then my husband would see't — I don't know what to do — But yet i'vads I'll try, so I will — for I will not send this letter to poor Master Horner, come what will on't.

COYOTE ON A FENCE

Bruce Graham

Shawna, 40s – 50s
Present, southern United States

Shawna vents about the electric company and capital punishment.

SHAWNA. Usta' be — 'fore they switched to the needle — when we still had the chair? — the lights would dim. No shit — just like in them old Bogart movies, they'd go . . . *(She illustrates.)* Zzzzzzzzzzz . . . then come back up. That's 'cause they were workin' off the prison generator 'cause — and this is such bullshit — the electric company didn't wanta be . . . fuck, what's the word — you better quit feedin' me drinks — they didn't want nothin' to do with it, and they — PARTICIPANT — that's it — that's the word — they didn't wanta be a participants in an execution. Is that bullshit or what — packa' fuckin' thieves like the 'lectric company gettin' all righteous. I mean, I don't know what you pay, but my bill . . . fuckin' thieves. Hypocrites — 'cause they're all for it — hell, everybody 'round here's for it 'cept for a couple of them crazies out front with their goddam candles and their . . . like we enjoy this, right? *(Loses her train of thought.)* Fucking electric company! They want guys executed but don't want people thinkin' they're responsible — like they're gonna' boycott the product or somethin'. We're not talkin' 'bout sneakers or . . . beer or somethin'. It's the 'lectric company, they got ya by the balls and they know it.

COYOTE ON A FENCE

Bruce Graham

Shawna, 40s – 50s
Present, southern United States

Shawna, tired and washed out, talks, but not for free.

SHAWNA. Goddam madhouse tonight. Never seen it like that — never. All them TV trucks? Never seen a crowd like that — nope . . . not even for Willie T. and he had a big one . . . but tonight . . . damn . . . *(Sipping her bottle of Bud.)* Man, this beats the shit outta that generic stuff I gotta tell ya. This is your expense account, right? . . . must be nice . . . *(Lighting a cigarette.)* Hey — you said "no names." No, I'm serious — no names. 'Cause after that goddamned BBC thing the Super reamed our asses and — don't bullshit me. 'Cause I'll tell you, you reporters are a pretty sleazy group yourself. Hell, I work with murderers and I gotta put ya all in the top three: murderers, lawyers, and reporters. So no names — I'm not gettin' in trouble for you people. *(Studying the Reporter.)* All right . . . long as it's just for "the record." But it better not get out. *(She takes a drink.)* Okay: Shawna DuChamps — small "u." Nahh, hell, I don't mind: forty-eight. Divorced. Joley DuChamps. Left me for another man: Jack Daniels. Three kids — two real good — Joley, Jr. I wanta kill sometimes. Been a correctional officer since I was twenty, which means in a couple years I'll have my thirty and I am gettin' the fuck out. I don't care — Burger King if I have to. If I could fit in one'a them little skirts I'd work here . . . So, the drinks're on you, right? Maybe an order of wings too? 'Cause there's a lotta reporters wanted ta talk to me tonight and I ain't talkin' for free . . .

CYMBELINE
William Shakespeare

Imogen, 20s – 30s

Imogen, in a daze, finds a headless man.

IMOGEN. Yes sir, to Milford-Haven, which is the way?
      I thank you: by yond bush? pray, how far thither?
      'Ods pittikins: can it be six mile yet?
      I have gone all night: faith, I'll lie down and sleep.
      But, soft! no bedfellow! O gods and goddesses!
      (Seeing the body of Cloten.)
      These flowers are like the pleasures of the world;
      This bloody man, the care on't. I hope I dream:
      For so I thought I was a cave-keeper,
      And cook to honest creatures. But 'tis not so:
      'Twas but a bolt of nothing, shot at nothing,
      Which the brain makes of fumes. Our very eyes
      Are sometimes like our judgements, blind. Good faith,
      I tremble still with fear: but if there be
      Yet left in heaven as small a drop of pity
      As a wren's eye, fear'd gods, a part of it!
      The dream's here still: even when I wake it is
      Without me, as within me: not imagin'd, felt.
      A headless man? The garments of Posthumus?
      I know the shape of's leg: this is his hand:
      His foot Mercurial: his Martial thigh:
      The brawns of Hercules: but his Jovial face —
      Murder in heaven! How — ? 'Tis gone. Pisanio,
      All curses madded Hecuba gave the Greeks,
      And mine to boot, be darted on thee! Thou,
      Conspir'd with that irregulous devil, Cloten,
      Hast here cut off my lord. To write, and read
      Be henceforth treacherous! Damn'd Pisanio

Hath with his forged letters (damn'd Pisanio.)
From this most bravest vessl of the world
Struck the main-top! O Posthumus, alas,
Where is thy head? where's that? Ay me! where's
        that?
Pisanio might have kill'd thee at the heart,
And left this head on. How should this be, Pisanio?
'Tis he, and Cloten: malice and lucre in them
Have laid this woe here. O, 'tis pregnant, pregnant!
The drug he gave me, which he said was precious
And cordial to me, have I not found it
Murd'rous to th' senses? That confirms it home:
This is Pisanio's deed, and Cloten — O!
Give colour to my pale cheek with thy blood,
That we the horrider may seem to those
Which chance to find us. O, my lord! my lord!

CYMBELINE

William Shakespeare

Imogen, 20s – 30s

After a long journey, Imogen stops to take a rest.

IMOGEN. I see a man's life is a tedious one,
      I have tir'd myself: and for two nights together
      Have made the ground my bed. I should be sick,
      But that my resolution helps me: Milford,
      When from the mountain-top Pisanio show'd thee,
      Thou was within a ken. O Jove! I think
      Foundations fly the wretched: such, I mean,
      Where they should be reliev'd. Two beggars told me
      I could not miss my way. Will poor folks lie,
      That have afflictions on them, knowing 'tis
      A punishment, or trial? Yes; no wonder,
      When rich ones scarce tell true. To lapse in fulness
      Is sorer than to lie for need: and falsehood
      Is worse in kings than beggars. My dear lord,
      Thou art one o' th' false ones! Now I think on thee,
      My hunger's gone; but even before, I was
      At point to sink, for food. — But what is this?
      Here is a path to 't: 'tis some savage hold:
      I were best not call; I dare not call: yet famine,
      Ere clean it o'erthrow Nature, makes it valiant.
      Plenty and peace breeds cowards: hardness ever
      Of hardiness is mother. Ho! who's here?
      If any thing that's civil, speak: if savage,
      Take, or lend. Ho! No answer? Then I'll enter.
      Best draw my sword; and if mine enemy
      But fear the sword like me, he'll scarcely look on't.
      Such a foe, good heavens!

A DAY IN THE DEATH OF JOE EGG
Peter Nichols

Sheila, 20s — 30s
1967, England

She is generously built, serious, and industrious. She enters carrying a small makeup bag. She addresses the audience.

SHEILA. One of these days I'll hit him. Honestly. *(She attends to her makeup, looking at the audience.)* He thinks because he throws a tantrum I'm going to stay home comforting him and miss the rehearsal and let them all down. He thinks he's only got to cry to get all he wants. I blame his mother. She gave him the kind of suffocating love that makes him think the world revolved around him, but because he's too intelligent to believe it really, he gets into these paddies and depressions. And when he's in one of those, he'll do anything to draw attention to himself. That spider on his face — you saw that. And all this stuff about Freddie. And yet it was Brian made me join these amateurs in the first place; he said I needed to get out more, have a rest from Joe. But she's no trouble. It's Brian. I don't know which is the greatest baby. Watching somebody as limited as Joe over ten years, I've begun to feel she's only one kind of cripple. Everybody's damaged in some way. There's a limit to what we can do. Brian, for instance, he goes so far — and hits the ceiling. Just can't fly any higher. Then he drops to the floor and we get self-pity again — despair. I'm sure, though, if he could go further — he could be a marvelous painter. That's another reason I said I'd join the amateurs: the thought that he'd be forced to go upstairs several nights a week and actually put paint on a canvas. And even if he *isn't* any good, he seems to need some work he can be proud of. Something to take his mind off his jealousy of anyone or anything I take to — relatives, friends, pets — even pot plants. I'm sure it's because they take up time he thinks I could be devoting to him. And Joe, of course, Joe, most of all, poor love. *(She rises, a thought bringing her back.)* Look, you mustn't assume I feel like this in the ordinary way. And even when I *am* a bit down, I shouldn't normally talk about it to a lot of complete strangers. But all this childish temper over Freddie — this showing off — it's more than I can stand. It makes me boil, honestly! Wouldn't you feel the same? That's why I'm telling you all this. A lot of total strangers. But wouldn't it make *you* boil? Honestly! A grown man jealous of poor Joe . . .

A DAY IN THE DEATH OF JOE EGG

Peter Nichols

Sheila, 20s — 30s
1967, England

Sheila, frustrated with Brian, addresses the audience.

SHEILA. I join in these jokes to please him. If it helps him live with her, I can't see the harm, can you? He hasn't any faith she's ever going to improve. Where I have, you see. I believe, even if she *showed* improvement, Bri wouldn't notice. He's dense about faith — faith isn't believing in fairy tales, it's being in a receptive frame of mind. I'm always on the lookout for some sign. One day when she was — what? — about twelve months old, I suppose, she was lying on the floor kicking her legs about and I was doing the flat. I'd made a little tower of four coloured bricks — plastic bricks — on a rug near her head. I got on with my dusting and when I looked again I saw she knocked it down. I put the four bricks up again and this time watched her. First her eyes, usually moving in all directions, must have glanced in passing at this bright tower. Then the arm that side began to show real signs of intention — and her fist started clenching and — spreading — with effort. The other arm — held here like that — *(Raising one bent arm to shoulder level.)* didn't move. At all. You see the importance — she was using for the first time one arm instead of both. Must have taken — I should think — ten minutes — strenuous labour — to reach them with her fingers — then her hand jerked in a spasm and she pulled down the tower again. *(Re-living the episode, she puts her hands over her face to regain composure.)* I can't tell you what it was like. But you can imagine, can't you? Several times the hand very nearly touched and got jerked away by spasm — and she'd try again. That was the best of it — she had a will, she had a mind of her own. Soon as Bri came home, I told him. I think he said something stupid like — you know — "That's great, put her down for piano lessons." But when he tested her — putting piles of bricks all along the circle of her reach — both arms — and even sometimes out of reach so that she had to stretch to get there

— well, of course, he saw it was true. It wasn't *much* to wait for — one arm movement completed — and even that wasn't surefire. She'd fall asleep, the firelight would distract her, sometimes the effort would bring on a fit. But more often than not she'd manage — and a vegetable couldn't have done that. Visitors never believed it. They hadn't the patience to watch so long. And it amazed me — I remember being stunned — when I realized they thought I shouldn't deceive myself. For one thing, it wasn't deception — and anyway what else could I do? We got very absorbed in the daily games. Found her coloured balls and bells and a Kelly — those clowns that won't lie down. Then she caught some bug and was very sick — had fit after fit — the Grand Mal, not the others — what amounted to a complete relapse. When she was over it, we tried the bricks again, but she couldn't even seem to see them. That was when Bri lost interest in her. I still try, though of course I don't bother telling him. I'll tell him when something happens. It seems to me only common sense. If she did it once, she could again. I think while there's life there's hope, don't you? I wonder if he ever imagines what she'd be like if her brain worked. *I* do. And Bri's mother always says: "Wouldn't she be lovely if she was running about?" Which makes Bri hoot with laughter. But I think of it too. Perhaps it's being a woman.

A DAY IN THE DEATH OF JOE EGG

Peter Nichols

Pam, 20s — 30s
1967, England

She dresses well, mispronounces her words in an upper-class gabble, and her posture and manners have been taken from fashionable magazines. She is blasé. She addresses the audience.

PAM. It wasn't my idea coming back here in the first place. But once Freddie's set eyes on a lame dog, you might as well talk to the moon. I keep looking at that door and thinking she's going to come through it any moment with that poor weirdie. I know it's awful but it's one of my — you know — THINGS. We're none of us perfect — I can't stand anything N.P.A. — Non Physically Attractive. Old women in bathing suits — and skin diseases — and cripples — and Rowton House–looking men who spit and have hair growing out of their ears. No good. I just can't look at them. I know Freddie's right about Hitler and of course that's horrid. Still, I can't help sympathising with Brian, can you? I don't mean the way he described. I think it should be done by the state. And so should charity. Then we might have an end of all those hideous dolls in shop doorways with irons on their legs . . . Freddie won't hear of it, of course. But then he loves a lame dog. Every year he buys so many tickets for the spastic raffle he wins a TV set and every year he gives it to an old folks' home. He used to try taking me along on his visits but I said it wasn't me at all and he gave up. One — place — we went, there were these poor freaks with — oh, you know — enormous heads and so on — and you just feel: Oh, put them out of their misery. Well, they wouldn't have survived in nature, it's only modern medicine, so modern medicine should be allowed to do away with them. A committee of doctors and do-gooders, naturally, to make sure there's no funny business, and then — if I say gas chamber that makes it sound horrid — but I do mean put to sleep. When Freddie gets all mealymouthed about it, I say: "Look, darling, if one of our kids was dying and they had a cure and you knew it had been discovered in the Nazi laboratories, would you refuse to let them use it?" I certainly wouldn't. I love my own immediate family and that's all. Can't cope with anymore. I want to go home and see them again. They may not be the most hard-working, well-behaved geniuses on earth but no one in their right mind could say they were N.P.A.

DREAM GIRL

Elmer Rice

Georgina, 20s – 30s
1945, New York City

Georgina talks to us about her dreams.

GEORGINA. All right. I'm ready. In sickness and in health. In joy and
in sorrow. Until death — No, no! Stop it, Georgina! You mustn't go on
like this! You mustn't. I'm at it again — drugging myself with dreams.
And when I come to, all I'll get from him is a slap in the face. He doesn't
care a damn for me. He's just having fun with me — just giving me the
runaround, that's all. He's calling up to find out if he won his bet on
Wilinski — that means more to him than I do. *(Springing to her feet.)*
No, I can't take it! I'll never see him again. I'll go before he gets back. I'll —
I'll — oh, I don't know. Anything — anything not to hear the bitter truth
from him.

ELECTRA

Sophokles, Translated by Carl Mueller

Electra, 20s – 30s
Ancient Greece

Electra tells us about her pain.

ELECTRA. Divine light,
    Sweet air,
    Again hear
    My pain.
    Divine light,
    Sweet air,
    Again hear
    My pain.
    Have you not witnessed when morning breaks
    My heart break, my heart break?
    When night falls, I do not feast
    In this house of ghosts.
    I lie alone.
    My father's dead.
    He did not die in war.
    He does not lie on a foreign shore.
    Here, at home,
    My mother's hands turned red
    With his blood. Adulteress,
    Adulterer, she and Aegisthus,
    Split him open with an axe.
    The tree fell,
    And father, I am left to dwell
    Alone in your house, my back
    Against the wall,
    Weeping for my father dead,
    Mourning my dead father.

But I swear, while my eyes see
The sun or stars in the sky,
I will never cease to cry out
My pain and my complaint.
I will be like the poor nightingale
Who killed her young,
Then sorrow raped her heart.
That is the song I will spill
Through this house where blood was spilt.
I call upon Persephone,
I call upon the dead,
I call upon the Furies,
Revenge my father's blood-stained marriage bed,
Revenge my father,
Send me back my brother,
I can no longer stomach the size of my sorrow.

AN EXPERIMENT WITH
AN AIR PUMP

Shelagh Stephenson

Isobel, 40s – 50s
1999, England

Isobel reads through a letter she has just written.

ISOBEL. "Loving words as I do, I now find my vocabulary insufficient to describe my anguish. How may I explain to you my fall from contentment to despair? I was never a loved thing; it was not a condition I had ever known. Recently, and most fleetingly, I discovered the rapture of that state. Now I know it to have been a fiction. My life stretches before me, and it is now a bitter road. All pleasure's pale now that I have felt love and may never feel it again. You will say that it was not a real love, and I would agree. It was a lie and it was moonshine, but how happy I was to bathe in its watery glow. Now my mouth is full of ashes. He caused dreams in me where none had thrived before, and I am without hope or consolation. Isobel Bridie" *(Isobel folds the letter.)*

FAT MEN IN SKIRTS
Nicky Silver

Phyllis, 40s
1990s, New York

Phyllis tells us about a recurring dream.

PHYLLIS. Lately, I have been having a recurring dream. When I was a little girl, we lived in a part of Philadelphia called Society Hill. In an apartment. Down the hall from us lived Mr. Antonelli. Mr. Antonelli worked at the Museum of Natural History. And he was big. He was a big man. Must've weighed three hundred pounds. He was the fattest human being I'd ever seen, close up. But he was well-groomed. And on certain nights of the week, Saturdays, I think, Saturdays mostly and Thursdays, Mr. Antonelli would dress as a woman and go wherever three-hundred-pound men who dress as women go, to seek whatever they can mistake for love. He'd put on a skirt and a blouse, sometimes a mumu-Bloody-Mary-type thing. And a lot of makeup. He wore a wig, a reddish kind of Ethel Merman affair. And always lovely matching jewelry sets: green rhinestone earrings, green rhinestone bracelets, brooches. He got all dolled up and went off to seek others like himself (although I can't imagine there were many others like Mr. Antonelli; three-hundred-pound transvestites are pretty much on their own in the world, I should think). When I was six, I was going to a friend's birthday party one Saturday, and I was wearing the sweetest little powder-blue jumper, and Mr. Antonelli got into the elevator with my mother and me. He looked down at me — this great mountain of gelatinous white flesh, and said, "My goodness, what a sweet little blue dress you have on." And I said, "You could borrow it sometime, if you want, Mr. Antonelli." I was six, and the concept of Junior and Misses sizing had not yet been made clear to me. Well, my mother squeezed my hand so tightly I thought my fingers would snap off. Once on the street, she explained to me that I must never, ever speak to Mr. Antonelli again. If he spoke to me, I was to nod politely. But I was never — under any circumstances — to speak to him again. And I was certainly not to get into the elevator with him. My mother explained to me that Mr. Antonelli was a freak. That he should be locked up. Forgotten about. That Mr. Antonelli, although not to blame him for his condition, was nevertheless, the lowest form of the species, a creature to fear, and his parents, poor souls, must have a terrible burden to bear.

Now. In my dream, I'm a little girl again. And I'm wearing my little powder-blue jumper. The one I wore that day. Only, I'm not on my way to any birthday party. I'm on a field trip with my class from school. We're at the zoo. Riding the monorail and laughing. The sun is shining, balloons fill the sky and we have cotton candy for lunch. We go to the reptile house and the polar-bear cage and the tigers are sunning themselves. Then we go to the monkey house. But there aren't any monkeys. There are, climbing the jungle gym, picking salt from their hair, dozens and dozens of fat men in skirts. Huge fat men, with matching jewelry sets, swinging from limb to limb, laughing in no language. And everyone laughs and points. And then they turn around. All the monkeys. All the men, turn around at once. They turn around and look at me, right at me. And they all have the same face. And it's Bishop's face. They all have my son's face.

GOOD NIGHT DESDEMONA (GOOD MORNING JULIET)

Anne-Marie MacDonald

Constance, 20s – 30s
Present

Constance projects wildly into the future.

CONSTANCE. Regina. I hate the prairies. They're flat. It's an absolute nightmare landscape of absolutes and I'm a relativist, I'll go mad. Diamonds are a girl's best friend. Diamonds are harder than a bed of nails. I can't feel anything. I'm perfectly fine. I'll call the Dean and resign. I'll go back to my apartment and watch the plants die and let the cats copulate freely. I'll order in groceries. Eventually I'll be evicted. I'll smell really bad and swear at people on the subway. Five years later I run into Professor Night and Ramona: They don't recognize me. I'm selling pencils. They buy one. Suddenly, I drop dead. They discover my true identity. I'm awarded my doctorate posthumously. Professor Night dedicates his complete works to me and lays roses on my grave every day. My stone bears a simple epithet: "Oh what a noble mind is here o'erthrown." . . . There's no time to lose! I have to start right now if I'm going to sink that low in five years. (*Grabs phone, dials.*) Hello, give me the office of the Dean! . . . Oh yes, I'll hold. (*While holding, she surveys the objects on her desk, picks them up one by one, addresses them, then tosses them into the wastebasket.*) The bronze wings that my Brownie pack gave me. (*Reads inscription.*) "To the best Brown Owl in the forest." I flew up more girls than any Brown Owl other than Lady Baden Powell. (*Toss. Picks up a jar that contains something like an anchovy.*) My appendix. It was removed in the summer of love when the rest of my family went to Expo '67. The doctor gave it to me in this baby food jar. He thought it would cheer me up. It did. (*Toss. Takes the plumed fountain pen from behind her ear.*) The fountain pen I made from my parakeet, Laurel. She used to sing "Volare."

She fell five stories and died instantly. (*Goes to toss it away, but cannot bear to do so. She replaces it behind her ear, where it stays for the rest of the play. Picks up the Manuscript.*) And this — my fool's gold. Silent mocking oracle. I'll do the world a favour.

GOOD NIGHT DESDEMONA (GOOD MORNING JULIET)

Anne-Marie MacDonald

Constance, 20s – 30s
Present

Here, Constance expresses her feelings about the men in Shakespeares plays.

CONSTANCE. Thank God they think that I'm a man.
    (*To God.*) Thank you. O thank you.
    How long can I avoid their locker room?
    Those guys remind me of the Stratford shows I've seen,
    where each production has a Roman bath:
    the scene might be a conference of state,
    but steam will rise and billow from the wings,
    while full-grown men in Velcro loincloths speak,
    while snapping towels at each other.
    Why is it Juliet's scenes with her Nurse
    are never in a sauna. Or *King Lear:*
    imagine Goneril and Regan, steaming
    as they plot the downfall of their Dad,
    while tearing hot wax from each other's legs;
    Ophelia, drowning in a whirlpool full
    of naked women. Portia, pumping iron —
    (*Verge of tears.*) I want to go home.
    I want to see my cats. I want to read
    Jane Eyre again and never leave the house.
    Where's the Fool? Where's the damn Fool?!
    How come I end up doing all his work?
    I should have waited in the wings
    for him to leap on stage and stop the fight,
    and then I could have pinned him down

and forced him to reveal the Author's name!
The Author — who must know my true identity.
The Author! Who — I have to pee . . .
There must be a convent around here somewhere.

HAMLET

William Shakespeare

Ophelia, 20s

Ophelia, filled with grief, tells us about it.

OPHELIA. O, what a noble mind is here o'erthrown!
       The courtier's, soldier's, scholar's, eye, tongue, sword,
       Th'expectancy and rose of the fair state,
       The glass of fashion and the mould of form,
       Th'observ'd of all observers, quite, quite down!
       And I, of ladies most deject and wretched,
       That suck'd the honey of his music vows,
       Now see that noble and most sovereign reason
       Like sweet bells jangled out of tune and harsh,
       That unmatch'd form and feature of blown youth
       Blasted with ecstasy. O woe is me
       T'have seen what I have seen, see what I see.

HOW I LEARNED TO DRIVE

Paula Vogel

Li'l Bit, 20s – 30s
Present, Maryland

Li'l Bit lets us in.

LI'L BIT. There were a lot of rumors about why I got kicked out of that fancy school in 1970. Some say I got caught with a man in my room. Some say as a kid on scholarship I fooled around with a rich man's daughter. *(Li'l Bit smiles innocently at the audience.)*

I'm not talking.

But the real truth was I had a constant companion in my dorm room — who was less than discrete. Canadian V.O. A fifth a day.

1970. A Nixon recession. I slept on the floors of friends who were out of work themselves. Took factory work when I could find it. A string of dead-end day jobs that didn't last very long.

What I did, most nights, was cruise the Beltway and the back roads of Maryland, where there was still country, past the battlefields and farmhouses. Racing in a 1965 Mustang — and as long as I had gasoline for my car and whiskey for me, the nights would pass. Fully tanked, I would speed past the churches and the trees on the bend, thinking just one notch of the steering wheel would be all it would take, and yet some . . . reflex took over. My hands on the wheel in the nine and three o'clock position — I never so much as got a ticket. He taught me well.

HOW I LEARNED TO DRIVE
Paula Vogel

Li'l Bit, 20s – 30s
Present, Maryland

Here, Li'l Bit tells us how she copes.

LI'L BIT. That day was the last day I lived in my body. I retreated above the neck, and I've lived inside the "fire" in my head ever since.

And now that seems like a long, long time ago. When we were both very young.

And before you know it, I'll be thirty-five. That's getting up there for a woman. And I find myself believing in things that a younger self vowed never to believe in. Things like family and forgiveness.

I know I'm lucky. Although I still have never known what it feels like to jog or dance. Anything that . . . "jiggles." I do like to watch people on the dance floor, or out on the running paths, just jiggling away. And I say — good for them. *(Li'l Bit moves to the car with pleasure.)*

The nearest sensation I feel — of flight in the body — I guess I feel when I'm driving. On a day like today. It's five A.M. The radio says it's going to be clear and crisp. I've got five hundred miles of highway ahead of me — and some back roads too. I filled the tank last night, and had the oil checked. Checked the tires, too. You've got to treat her . . . with respect.

First thing I do is: Check under the car. To see if any two-year-olds or household cats have crawled beneath, and strategically placed their skulls behind my back tires. *(Li'l Bit crouches.)*

Nope. I get in the car. *(Li'l Bit does so.)*

I lock the doors. And turn the key. Then I adjust the most important control on the dashboard — the radio —

HOW I LEARNED TO DRIVE
Paula Vogel

Li'l Bit, 20s – 30s
Present, Maryland

Li'l Bit describes what it was like.

LI'L BIT. Sometimes to tell a secret, you first have to teach a lesson. We're going to start our lesson tonight on an early, warm summer evening.

In a parking lot overlooking the Beltsville Agricultural Farms in suburban Maryland.

Less than a mile away, the crumbling concrete of U.S. One wends its way past one-room revival churches, the porno drive-in, and boarded-up motels with For Sale signs tumbling down.

Like I said, it's a warm summer evening.

Here on the land the Department of Agriculture owns, the smell of sleeping farm animal is thick on the air. The smells of clover and hay mix in with the smells of the leather dashboard. You can still imagine how Maryland used to be, before the malls took over. This countryside was once dotted with farmhouses — from their porches you could have witnessed the Civil War raging in the front fields.

Oh yes. There's a moon over Maryland tonight, that spills into the car where I sit beside a man old enough to be — did I mention how still the night is? Damp soil and tranquil air. It's the kind of night that makes a middle-aged man with a mortgage feel like a country boy again.

It's 1969. And I am very old, very cynical of the world, and I know it all. In short, I am seventeen years old, parking off a dark lane with a married man on an early summer night.

AN IDEAL HUSBAND

Oscar Wilde

Mrs. Cheveley, 30s – 40s
1800s, England

Mrs. Cheveley spies a letter.

MRS. CHEVELEY. I wonder what woman he is waiting for tonight. It will be delightful to catch him. Men always look so silly when they are caught. And they are always being caught. *(Looks about the room and approaches the writing table.)* What a very interesting room! What a very interesting picture! Wonder what his correspondence is like. *(Takes up letters.)* Oh, what a very uninteresting correspondence! Bills and cards, debts and dowagers! Who on earth writes to him on pink paper? How silly to write on pink paper! It looks like the beginning of a middle-class romance. Romance should never begin with sentiment. It should begin with science and end with a settlement. *(Puts letter down, then takes it up again.)* I know that handwriting. That is Gertrude Chiltern's. I remember it perfectly. The ten commandments in every stroke of the pen, and the moral law all over the page. Wonder what Gertrude is writing to him about? Something horrid about me, I suppose. How I detest that woman! *(Reads it.)* "I trust you. I want you. I am coming to you. Gertrude." "I trust you. I want you. I am coming to you."

INDEPENDENCE

Lee Blessing

Kess, 30s
Present, Independence, Iowa

Kess tells us what it was like.

KESS. *Mom . . . (But Evelyn is gone. Kess waits a beat, then goes on in a loud voice.)* I hated the woods. I hated the birds and the trees and spiders and . . . ticks. But when you're sixteen, and you want a lover — and it has to be a girl or you wouldn't be in love — you have to become a YWCA counselor and go to the woods. And just hope some other YWCA counselor is there for the same reason. And pray that people don't find out about you and fire you because they think you want to sleep with eight-year-old campers or something. I spent three summers lying terrified in a pup tent for one affair that lasted two weeks, with a counselor I didn't even like. *(A beat.)* Mom? I know you can hear me.

INVITATION TO A MARCH
Arthur Laurents

Camilla, 40s
Present, Long Island, New York

Camilla tells us about her family history.

CAMILLA. *(Front.)* Hello. I'm Camilla Jablonski. I'd like to welcome you to the South Shore of Long Island. I love it here: You can breathe. Take a breath. Go on, take a big one. Don't be afraid; the air is still good here. Besides, it's summer, and who can be afraid of anything in summer? *(She takes off her hat.)* This house used to be on my father's farm. Thirty-five years ago he was hoodwinked into buying a half-mile of these dunes sight unseen. He thought he was getting a kingdom of farmland, but in those days the whole kit and kaboodle of beach wasn't worth a pile of — I don't know you well enough yet. So, he hired out as a hand, and scrimped and saved all over again. Still, it took me, my four brothers, and one helluva depression to get the old man his farm. By the time he died — eighty-three he was, with his hair still red and his fist still shaking — this beach was worth ten farms. Think he cared? Not two hoots and a holler in hell. A farm was what he wanted, a farm was what he got. But everything's changing so fast: That wonderful old man's farm is part of an air base now and I had the house moved across our local Mason-Dixon line. That's the big highway out there. North are the truck farmers and the handymen. South: the commuters, summer people — and now: us. But there she is, sitting pretty on these dunes. And there you are, sitting pretty in the ocean. Don't worry, the tide is out.

JENNY KEEPS TALKING
Richard Greenberg

Jenny, 20s – 30s
1990, New York City

Jenny's just been fired.

JENNY. I have no fucking boxes! *(Beat.)*

I mean — am I expected to return tomorrow with cartons that I collect tonight as I pass by the local liquor stores on my way home? The least they could do is supply you with . . . *(Beat.)*

Someone could come to my door, perhaps. Notice, no one has. But someone could possibly come to my door now. And knock. "Jenny, I have a box in my office that I keep old notebooks in, please take it. And Jenny — You Don't Deserve This!" And then I could ask them: "Do I deserve this?" I would ask them. Her. I would ask her, genuinely, "Do I deserve this?" *(Beat. She snaps out of it. She throws something into something.)*

So I walk in and was immediately greeted by this . . . shocking congruence of bared teeth. Doug's and Buckman's. Too grotesque even to be called *false* smiles. And, in that instant, I knew two things: 1) It was happening, and 2) I had in no way expected it to happen. *(Beat. She empties one of the containers.)*

So Buckman drizzled on some nonsense about "preserving the *spirit* of the newspaper by *revamping* the paper's personnel." I, of course, fixed on Doug — thinking — thinking, Here — here will be my salvation, *some* salvation — and finally Buckman's idiocy quieted down and I was still staring at Doug and so he felt — he felt compelled to say something. And he cleared his throat. And in a perfectly smooth voice, said to me — to his spiritual kin, adulterous former-lover, age-old friend, ideological compatriot — he said, "We're so terribly sorry, Jenny. But one thing's for sure — with a talent like yours, there's no need to worry." *(Beat.)*

And I thought, "Well, this was the man I supposed to be a rough-and-ready warrior in an impure world. But now, I see, his words have become sepulchres." *(Beat.)*

And so I said to him, "Your words have become sepulchres." And I walked out of that room. And came here. *(Beat.)*

And began my quest for some fucking, fucking, fucking *boxes* to pack my life away in. *(Beat.)*

JENNY KEEPS TALKING

Richard Greenberg

Claudia, 20s – 30s
1990s, New York City

Claudia shares her predicament with us.

CLAUDIA. I have so much to tell you, I have such wonderful plans! Oh, but my heart's still racing, I bet you can hear it — I mean, I turn the corner, and there's the nephew, and he sees me, and he says, "Excuse me, aren't you Miss — ?" And I say to him, "Sorry, can't talk, I have bundles" and beeline it over here, but that one was close, really *close. (She unpacks bundles, puts things away, makes herself tea, et cetera: business.)* I mean, It's only a matter of time, anyway, I mean, the clock is *ticking.* This isn't my apartment, this apartment belongs to Eliot Ashkenazi. The Junior Editor at Houghton Mifflin? *(No recognition from us.)* No, of course not, why should you? So, umm, anyway, it's an illegal sublet, and Eliot Ashkenazi, who pays two-hundred-and-forty dollars a month, says to me before he goes away, "Whatever you do, don't leave your message on the machine, or the landlord could find out and kick me out." But tell me, when has that ever happened? That the landlord's just *called up?* Like, "Hey, Claude, how ya doin', it's the landlord?"

So, of course, I leave my message on the machine — anyway, Eliot Ashkenazi has this really dismal voice with this very ugly, backward placement, and it's an offense, that kind of voice, so the landlord calls. Something about three months back rent. And I'm crazed, because it's the worst possible time, also I don't know how to break it to Eliot Ashkenazi, who before he left was very, very intensely . . . concerned about this issue, and is impossible to reach, and, anyway, I think they're very stringent about what they let you say to them at the asylum. So, *ahime!* The sky is falling, the sky is falling . . . as it actually is. But I love the rain. "I always see myself dead in it." What's that from? *A Farewell to Arms.* I win. Five points for me. *(She crosses to window.)* The nephew is gone — ah-hah! No more worry, no more cares. Right?

JENNY KEEPS TALKING

Richard Greenberg

Grandma, 60s
1990s, New York City

Grandma shares with us about her marriage.

GRANDMA. I came to this family, terribly young — married a husband, terribly sweet, terribly old. Lethal people my husband's family. And here was this large girl with swarthy, large parents. A mistake. Terrible mistake. Nice marriage, though. Swift at any rate. Quietly lethal people. I was too new-fangled. Well, they'd seen the Civil *War*, for God's — don't know how they felt about the outcome, though. Have my suspicions. *(Sips sherry.)* Never raised their voices, that bunch. Very effective. So much easier to be vicious that way. I've become, mmmm, terribly fond of "measured tones."

Invented my accent.

Invented my voice.

My, mmmm, vocabulary.

After a while, it's all the same. Live inside it. No problem. Let's see. *(Pulls two sheets of paper from portfolio, puts on glasses, reds.)*

"Dear . . . so-on-and-so-on . . .

Protect not only you, not only me, but protect Claudia from *herself*." *That's* melodrama. *(Reads from other letter.)*

"Dear . . . so-on-and-so-on . . .

This is my chance . . . my *real* chance . . ."

Whine, whine, whine.

Nice girl, though. Impossible, but darling. Well, *mine*. She used to stay with me from time to time, whenever, whenever, mmmm, *crisis* fell.

JENNY KEEPS TALKING

Richard Greenberg

Jenny, 20s – 30s
1990s, New York City

Jenny tells us about Buckman.

JENNY. So, last week, the day after the announcement — Buckman comes into the office and meets with all of us. He wants to assure us that he's *acquired* this paper because he *loves* this paper and wants to see it continue functioning *just* the *way* it *is*. And he smiles and he has these teeth and I'm thinking the Museum of Natural History is where this and his teeth belong; he should *acquire* the Museum of Natural History and go and live in one of the Dioramas, where his teeth will finally feel at home in this world. *(Beat.)* I mean, how does he smile, with all his billions, with his various empires, with his gilded villas, and awesome power, how does he smile, if with all that, he remains immune to modern dentistry? I ask you. *(Beat.)* But, really, I think Doug will save me. *(Beat.)* Save me! What's that? *(Beat.)* Doug is a good man. He's decent. Although, I have to say his behavior over the last few weeks has made me want to burn his effigy in Washington Square Park. But that's a phase. I mean, a phase of mine. Doug will stay the same. At least for Buckman's tenure at this newspaper — which, let's face it, will last as long as the newspaper lasts, because men like that — men like Buckman — the adjustment they make to mortality is to make sure everything *dies* with them. Like Pharoahs whose tombs were filled with all their worldly possessions. They don't have legacies; they don't *pass on*, they . . . liquidate. And so Doug will continue to appease, to mollify, to — well, to lie and corrupt essentially. But Doug is the kind of man who passes something on, who believes that a *soiled* legacy is at least *something*. Which alternately disgusts me and inspires me. *(Beat.)* So, Doug — Doug, really is about to enter the most compelling phase of his life. *(Beat.)* So, yippee for Doug, but where does that leave me? *(Beat.)*

THE JEW OF MALTA

Christopher Marlowe

Abigail, 20s

Frustrated, Abigail speaks to us.

ABIGAIL. Hard-hearted father, unkind Barabas,
      Was this the pursuit of thy policy?
      To make me show them favour severally,
      That by my favour they should both be slain?
      Admit thou lovedst not Lodowick for his sin,
      Yet Don Mathias ne'er offended thee:
      But thou wert set upon extreme revenge,
      Because the Prior dispossessed thee once,
      And couldst not venge it, but upon his son,
      Nor on his son, but by Mathias' means;
      Nor on Mathias, but by murdering me.
      But I perceive there is no love on earth,
      Pity in Jews, nor piety in Turks.
      But here comes cursed Ithamore with the friar.

JOAN OF LORRAINE
Maxwell Anderson

Joan, 20s
1600s, France

Joan asks for help.

JOAN. King of Heaven, I come to fulfill a vow. The truce with Burgundy is signed, we are at peace, I shall wear this white armor no more. I leave it here on your altar. We are at peace, my King, but not such a peace as we dreamed; no, horribly, evilly in armistice, with much of the war to be fought and our enemies preparing while we dwindle here from town to town, holding court, receiving embassies, and dismissing soldiers. From town to town, from city to city, I have attended, doing the King's bidding, for he asks me to stay beside him — and this is the king of Your choosing, Your regent in France. We have feasted in Campiegne, Senlis and Beauvais, and we must feast in many more, if the plans hold. — But, O King of Heaven, the food is bitter. It is bought with money the King has accepted in payment for provinces and cities. I would rather sleep on the ground again, and chew my handful of beans, and rise to face the rank of English spears. For this way we shall lose all we have won. Even I can see that, and my Voices have said nothing. — If my Voices would speak again — if they would tell me what I should do — then I could sleep at night and accept what comes to me. But they have not spoken, they are silent. And I ask again and again — may I go into battle, or must I remain with the King and his household, busy with the nothings that fill these days? If my Voices do not answer, if no injunction is laid on me, then I cannot stay here. I must arm again, and find the enemy, and fight as before. — Let my Voices speak to me if this is wrong! Let them speak now! I wait here alone, in the darkness and silence. — There is no answer. Have I been abandoned? Have I made an error that is not forgiven? — No answer still. — Then I must go into battle, King of Heaven. I shall find another armor, not this shining one in which I rode as Your messenger, but another, dark and humble, fitting to a common soldier. Whether I win or lose, it will be better than in these chattering rooms, trying to say something that means nothing. I think I have courage to die, but not to die thus, in small, sick ways, daily. — Is there a Voice then?

LADY WINDERMERE'S FAN

Oscar Wilde

Lady Windermere, 20s – 30s
1800s, England

Waiting for Lord Darlington, Lady Windermere runs through all her options.

LADY WINDERMERE. Why doesn't he come? This waiting is horrible. He should be here. Why is he not here, to wake by passionate words some fire within me? I am cold — cold as a loveless thing. Arthur must have read my letter by this time. If he cared for me, he would have come after me, would have taken me back by force. But he doesn't care. He's entrammelled by this woman — fascinated by her — dominated by her. If a woman wants to hold a man, she has merely to appeal to what is worst in him. We make gods of men and they leave us. Others make brutes of them and they fawn and are faithful. How hideous life is! . . . Oh! it was mad of me to come here, horribly mad. And yet, which is the worst, I wonder, to be at the mercy of a man who loves one, or the wife of a man who in one's own house dishonours one? What woman knows? What woman in the whole world? But will he love me always, this man to whom I am giving my life? What do I bring him? Lips that have lost the note of joy, eyes that are blinded by tears, chill hands and icy heart. I bring him nothing. I must go back — no; I can't go back, my letter has put me in their power — Arthur would not take me back! That fatal letter! No! Lord Darlington leaves England tomorrow. I will go with him — I have no choice.

LADY WINDERMERE'S FAN

Oscar Wilde

Lady Windermere, 20s – 30s
1800s, England

Unsure, Lady Windermere looks for answers.

LADY WINDERMERE. How horrible! I understand now what Lord Darlington meant by the imaginary instance of the couple not two years married. Oh! it can't be true — she spoke of enormous sums of money paid to this woman. I know where Arthur keeps his bank book — in one of the drawers of that desk. I might find out by that. I *will* find out. *(Opens drawer.)* No, it is some hideous mistake. Some silly scandal! He loves *me!* He loves *me!* But why should I not look? I am his wife, I have a right to look! *(Returns to bureau, takes out book and examines it, page by page, smiles and gives a sigh of relief.)* I knew it! there is not a word of truth in this stupid story. *(Puts book back in drawer. As she does so, starts and takes out another book.)* A second book — private — locked! *(Tries to open it, but fails. Sees paper knife on bureau, and with it cuts cover from book. Begins to start at the first page.)* "Mrs Erlynne — 600 — Mrs Erlynne — 700 — Mrs Erlynne — 400." Oh! it is true! it is true! How horrible!

LAKE HOLLYWOOD

John Guare

Young Girl, 14
1940, New Hampshire

THE YOUNG GIRL. *(To audience.)* Water comes next to air as a life necessity; it should be the best the earth affords. New Hampshire, the Granite State, has water power in abundance. Lake Winnipesaukee which in Indian means the Smile of the Great Spirit is eighty-five square miles of water. It offers natural beauty the like of which is unequaled anywhere in the world. The scent of pines. The glory of the clouds. The purity of the air. Come enjoy the exhilaration of bathing in the healing and invigorating water of a lake such as Winnipesaukee and become one with the smile of the Great Spirit.

LAUGHING WILD

Christopher Durang

Woman, Any age
Present, New York City

Here we hear about what happened in the supermarket.

WOMAN. I want to talk to you about life. It's just too difficult to be alive, isn't it, and to try to function? There are all these people to deal with. I tried to buy a can of tuna fish in the supermarket, and there was this *person* standing right in front of where I wanted to reach out to get the tuna fish, and I waited a while, to see if they'd move, and they didn't — they were looking at tuna fish too, but they were taking a real long time on it, reading the ingredients on each can like they were a book, a pretty boring book, if you ask me, but nobody has; so I waited a long while, and they didn't move, and I couldn't get to the tuna fish cans; and I thought about asking them to move, but then they seemed so stupid not to have *sensed* that I needed to get by them that I had this awful fear that it would do no good, no good at all, to ask them, they'd probably say something like, "We'll move when we're goddam ready, you nagging bitch," and then what would I do? And so then I started to cry out of frustration, quietly, so as not to disturb anyone, and still, even though I was softly sobbing, this stupid person didn't *grasp* that I needed to get by them to reach the goddam tuna fish, people are so insensitive, I just hate them, and so I reached over with my fist, and I brought it down real hard on his head and I screamed: "Would you kindly, move, asshole!!!"

And the person fell to the ground, and looked totally startled, and some child nearby started to cry, and I was still crying, and I couldn't imagine making use of the tuna fish now anyway, and so I shouted at the child to stop crying — I mean, it was drawing too much attention to me — and I ran out of the supermarket, and I thought, I'll take a taxi to the Metropolitan Museum of Art, I needed to be surrounded with culture right now, not tuna fish.

LUCIA MAD
Don Nigro

Lucia, Any age
1900s, England

Lucia, in the nuthouse, talks to us.

LUCIA. In the labyrinth of London the mad girl wanders, poor Irish rat in a maze, searching always for my love. At first I thought I'd avoid him, he'd learn from mutual friends I was in London, feel obliged to pay a call of friendship, and, once out from my parents' evil web of conspiracy against me I would seduce him, and he would be forever enslaved by his hunger for me. But he didn't show up. So I went looking for him, places I'd heard he would frequent, but kept just missing him, when I went to his lodgings, nobody was home, sometimes I'd hear boots clattering down the back stairs as I came up the front. I chased the demon all over London and never once caught sight of him. Then I got word he'd slipped quietly back to Paris. Slowly I crept, closer and closer, across the cold channel waters, through the back alleys of Paris, in a landscape of garbage cans and stray cats, wind in my face and fury in my soul, to find once again my beloved, my own, my destiny.

MACBETH

William Shakespeare

Lady Macbeth, 40s – 50s

Hearing that the King is due to arrive, Lady Macbeth tells of her plans.

LADY MACBETH. The raven himself is hoarse,
>That croaks the fatal entrance of Duncan
>Under my battlements. Come, you Spirits
>That tend on mortal thoughts, unsex me here,
>And fill me, from the crown to the toe, top-full
>Of direst cruelty! make thick my blood,
>Stop up th'access and passage to remorse;
>That no compunctious visitings of Nature
>Shake my fell purpose, nor keep peace between
>Th'effect and it! Come to my woman's breasts,
>And take my milk for gall, you murth'ring ministers,
>Wherever in your sightless substances
>You wait on Nature's mischief! Come, thick Night,
>And pall thee in the dunnest smoke of Hell,
>That my keen knife see not the wound it makes,
>Nor Heaven peep through the blanket of the dark,
>To cry, "Hold, hold!"

THE MAIDS

Jean Genet

Solange, 20s – 30s
1940s, France

Solange talks to us about Claire and Madame.

SOLANGE. Claire? She was really very fond of Madame. . . . YOUR dresses again! And THAT white dress, THAT one, which I forbade her to put on, the one you wore the night of the Opera Ball, the night you poked fun at her, because she was sitting in the kitchen admiring a photo of Gary Cooper. . . . Madame will remember. Madame will remember her gentle irony, the maternal grace with which she took the magazine from us, and smiled. Nor will Madame forget that she called her Clarinette. Monsieur laughed until the tears rolled down his cheeks. . . . Eh? Who am I? The monstrous soul of servantdom! . . . No, Inspector, I'll explain nothing in their presence. That's *our* business. It would be a fine thing if masters could pierce the shadows where servants live. . . . That, my child, is our darkness, ours. (*She lights a cigarette and smokes clumsily. The smoke makes her cough.*) Neither you nor anyone else will be told anything. Just tell yourselves that this time Solange has gone through with it. . . . You see her dressed in red. She is going out.

THE MAIDS

Jean Genet

Solange, 20s – 30s
1940s, France

Solange has just killed Madame. Or has he?

SOLANGE. Madame. . . . At last! Madame is dead! . . . laid out on the linoleum . . . strangled by the dish-gloves. What? Oh, Madame may remain seated. . . . Madame may call me Mademoiselle Solange. . . . Exactly. It's because of what I've done. Madame and Monsieur will call me Mademoiselle Solange Lemercier. . . . Madame should have taken off that black dress. It's grotesque. (*She imitates Madame's voice.*) So I'm reduced to wearing mourning for my maid. As I left the cemetery all the servants of the neighborhood marched past me as if I were a member of the family. I've so often been part of the family. Death will see the joke through to the bitter end. . . . What? Oh! Madame needn't feel sorry for me. I'm Madame's equal and I hold my head high.

THE MARRIAGE OF BETTE AND BOO

Christopher Durang

Bette, 30s
1980s, Somewhere in the United States

Bette calls an old friend.

BETTE. Hello, Bonnie? This is Betsy. Betsy. (*To remind her.*) Bonnie, your grade is eight, and Betsy, your grade is five. Yes, It's me. How are you? Oh, I'm sorry, I woke you? Well, what time is it? Oh I'm sorry. But isn't Florida in a different time zone than we are? Oh. I thought it was. Oh well.

Bonnie, are you married? How many children do you have? Two. That's nice. Are you going to have any more? Oh, I think you should. Yes, I'm married. To Boo. I wrote you. Oh, I never wrote you? How many years since we've spoken? Since we were fifteen. Well, I'm not a very good correspondent. Oh, dear, you're yawning, I guess it's too late to have called. Bonnie, do you remember the beach and little Jimmy Winkler? I used to dress him up as a lamp shade, it was so cute. Oh. Well, do you remember when Miss Willis had me stand in the corner, and you stand in the wastebasket, and then your grandmother came to class that day? I thought you'd remember that. Oh, you want to go back to sleep?

Oh, I'm sorry. Bonnie, before you hang up, I've lost two babies. No, I don't mean misplaced, stupid, they died. I go through the whole nine month period of carrying them, and then when it's over, they just take them away. I don't even see the bodies. Hello? Oh, I thought you weren't there. I'm sorry, I didn't realize it was so late. I thought Florida was Central time or something. Yes, I got twelve in geography or something, you remember? Betsy, your grade is twelve and Bonnie, your grade is . . . what did you get in geography? Well, it's not important anyway. What? No, Boo's not home. Well, sometimes he just goes to a bar and then he doesn't come home until the bar closes, and some of them don't close at all and

75

so he gets confused what time it is. Does your husband drink? Oh, that's good. What's his name? Scooter? Like bicycle? I like the name Scooter. I love cute things. Do you remember Jackie Cooper in *Skippy* and his best friend Sukey? I cried and cried. Hello, are you still there? I'm sorry, I guess I better let you go back to sleep. Good-bye, Bonnie, it was good to hear your voice. (*Hangs up.*)

MASTER CLASS

Terrence McNally

Maria, 40s – 50s
1980s, New York City

Maria tells us what she expects.

MARIA. No applause. We're here to work. You're not in a theater. This is a classroom. No folderol. This is a master class. Singing is serious business. We're going to roll up our sleeves and work. I appreciate your welcome but enough is enough. *Basta. Fini.* Eh? So. How is everyone? Can you hear me? I don't believe in microphones. Singing is first of all about projection. So is speech. People are forgetting how to listen. They want everything blasted at them. Listening takes concentration. If you can't hear me, it's your fault. You're not concentrating. I don't get any louder than this. So come down closer or leave. No takers? What? You're all scared of me? Eh? Is that it? I don't bite. I promise you. I bark, I bark quite a bit actually, but I don't bite. I don't know what you're expecting. What did they tell you? I hope you're not expecting me to sing. Well, we shall see what we shall see. *Allora*, so, let's begin.

MEASURE FOR MEASURE

William Shakespeare

Isabella, 20s – 30s

Isabella tells us about her dilemma.

ISABELLA.

> To whom shall I complain? Did I tell this,
> Who would believe me? O perilous mouths,
> That bear in them one and the self-same tongue
> Either of condemnation or approof!
> Bidding the law make court'sy to their will;
> Hooking both right and wrong to th'appetite,
> To follow as it draws! I'll to my brother.
> Though he hath fall'n by prompture of the blood,
> Yet hath he in him such a mind of honour.
> That had he twenty heads to tender down
> On twenty bloody blocks, he'd yield them up
> Before his sister should her body stoop
> To such abhorr'd pollution
> Then, Isabel live chaste, and brother, die:
> More than our brother is our chastity.
> I'll tell him yet of Angelo's request,
> And fit his mind to death, for his soul's rest.

MEDEA
Euripides, Translated by Carl Mueller

Nurse, Any age
Ancient Greece

What if?

NURSE. If only they had never gone! If the Argo's hull
      Never had winged out through the grey-blue jaws of rock
      And on towards Colchis! If that pine on Pelion's slopes
      Had never felt the axe, and fallen, to put oars
      Into those heroes' hands, who went at Pelias' bidding
      To fetch the golden fleece! Then neither would Medea,
      My mistress, ever have set sail for the walled town
      Of Iolcus, mad with love for Jason; nor would she,
      When Pelias' daughters, at her instance, killed their father,
      Have come with Jason and her children to live here
      In Corinth; where, coming as an exile, she has earned
      The citizens' welcome; while to Jason she is all
      Obedience — and in marriage that's the saving thing,
      When a wife obediently accepts her husband's will.

      But now her world has turned to enmity, and wounds her
      Where her affection's deepest. Jason has betrayed
      His own sons, and my mistress, for a royal bed,
      For alliance with the king of Corinth. He has married
      Glauce, Creon's daughter. Poor Medea! Scorned and shamed,
      She raves, invoking every vow and solemn pledge
      That Jason made her, and calls the gods as witnesses
      What thanks she has received for her fidelity.
      She will not eat; she lies collapsed in agony,
      Dissolving the long hours in tears. Since first she heard
      Of Jason's wickedness, she has not raised her eyes,
      Or moved her cheek from the hard ground; and when her friends

Reason with her, she might be a rock or wave of the sea,
For all she hears — unless, maybe, she turns away
Her lovely head, speaks to herself alone, and wails
Aloud for her dear father, her own land and home,
Which she betrayed and left, to come here with this man
Who now spurns and insults her. Poor Medea! Now
She learns through pain what blessings they enjoy who are not
Uprooted from their native land. She hates her sons:
To see them is no pleasure to her. I am afraid
Some dreadful purpose is forming in her mind. She is
A frightening woman; no one who makes an enemy
Of her will carry off an easy victory.

THE MEMORY OF WATER
Shelagh Stephenson

Catherine, 30s
Present, England

Catherine is desperate for a call from her boyfriend.

CATHERINE. Ring ring ring, please God, make him ring. Holy Mary Mother of God, I'll come back to the church, I'll do anything, make him ring now. Xavier, listen to me, pick up the fucking phone, please, I'm going off my head. I can't stand this. Why are you doing this to me? It's not fair. I'm getting an ulcer, you're making me ill. OK, I'm going to count to ten and then I'm going to phone you. If you haven't phoned by the time I've finished this joint I'm going to ring you, can you hear me? Just pick up the phone and speak to me. You could be dead for all I know, you could have had an accident or anything. Xavier, this is killing me.

MIDDLE OF THE NIGHT

Paddy Chayefsky

The Girl, 20s – 30s
1950s, New York City

Here, Betty speaks to Marilyn, finally.

THE GIRL. Where have you been, for Pete's sakes, Marilyn? This is Betty.
I must have called you twenty times. Wait a minute. I called you around
eleven o'clock. I called you every half hour on the half hour and it's three-
thirty now. Well, how's Frank and the kids? No, I'm at my mother's house.
Well, who told you? Oh, really, when was this? You mean George called
you at four o'clock in the morning? Then you know all about it. Listen
Marilyn, can I come over and stay with you for a couple of nights? I'll
sleep on the couch, but I'm over here at my mother's and I'm going out
of my mind. Well, when will Frank get home? I'm not blaming George,
Marilyn. Listen, he's a nice guy, but — I can't talk about it over the
phone, Marilyn. Can I come over and see you for a few minutes? Can I
come over after dinner then? Listen, I wouldn't ask you but I need to talk
to somebody — Oh, I'm sorry. How seriously sick is she? Well, give Frank
my best. No, no, no, it's all right, Marilyn. No, I'm all right, Marilyn.
No, it's — No, I'll call you late tonight. Sure — Okay, I'll see you.

A MIDSUMMER NIGHT'S DREAM

William Shakespeare

Helena, 20s – 30s
1600, England

*Helena, tall and beautiful. She is madly in love with Demetrius and plots
how to see him again.*

HELENA.

> How happy some o'er other some can be!
> Through Athens I am thought as fair as she.
> But what of that? Demetrius thinks not so;
> He will not know what all but he do know;
> And as he errs, doting on Hermia's eyes,
> So I, admiring of his qualities.
> Things base and vile, holding no quantity,
> Love can transpose to form and dignity.
> Love looks not with the eyes, but with the mind,
> And therefore is wing'd Cupid painted blind;
> Nor hath Love's mind of any judgement taste:
> Wings, and no eyes, figure unheedy haste.
> And therefore is Love said to be a child,
> Because in choice he is so oft beguil'd.
> As waggish boys, in game, themselves forswear,
> So the boy Love is perjur'd everywhere;
> For, ere Demetrius look'd on Hermia's eyne,
> He hail'd down oaths that he was only mine;
> And when this hail some heat from Hermia felt,
> So he dissolv'd, and show'rs of oaths did melt.
> I will go tell him of fair Hermia's flight:
> Then to the wood will he, tomorrow night,
> Pursue her; and for this intelligence
> If I have thanks, it is a dear expense.
> But herein mean I to enrich my pain,
> To have his sight thither and back again.

THE MINEOLA TWINS

Paula Vogel

Myra, 17
1950s, Mineola, NY

This bizarre dream.is Myra's

MYRA. So. It was like homeroom, only we were calculating the hypotenuse of hygiene. I whispered to Billy Bonnell — what does that mean?
And he said: Yuck-yuck — it's the same angle as the triangle under your
skirt, Myra Richards. Yuck-yuck.

Shut up Creep! Thhwwack! My metal straight edge took off the top
of his cranium. And then Mrs. Hopkins said, in this voice from the crypt:
Miss Richards — what is the hypotenuse of hygiene?

And just as I was saying Excuse Me, Mrs. Hopkins, But I Didn't
Know What the Homework Was for Today on Account of Being Sus-
pended Last Week By You 'Cause of the Dumb-Ass Dress Code —

The Voice Cuts In on the Intercom:

" . . . Get . . . To . . . The . . . Door . . . Now."

And we all got real scared. And the Nuclear Air Raid Siren Came
On, REAL LOUD. And kids started bawling and scrambling under their
desks. Somehow we knew it was For Real. We could hear this weird
whistling of the bombs coming for us, with a straight line drawn from
Moscow to Mineola. Dead Center for the Nassau County Court House.
Dead Center for Roosevelt Field. And Dead Center for Mineola High.
Home of the Mineola Mustangs.

And I knew it would do diddley-squat to get under the desk. Something drew me into the hall, where there was pulsing Red Light and Green
Smoke.

Like Christmas in Hell.

I just kept walking.

Kids' bodies were mangled everywhere. In the middle of the hall, Our
Principal Mr. Chotner was hypotenusing under Miss Dorothy Comby's
skirt.

I just kept walking.

The girls' Glee Club had spread-eagled Mr. Koch the driver's ed instructor further down the hall, and they were getting the long-handled custodian's broom out of the closet.

I just kept walking.

I checked my watch. Five minutes to the Apocalypse. I could hear the bombs humming louder now. I thought of crossing against the lights and getting home. But there's nothing lonelier than watching your parents hug while you curl up on the rug alone and Mom's ceramic dogs melt on the mantle as the sky glows its final Big Red.

Then I heard **The Voice** on the intercom say to me:

" **. . . Find . . . Her . . .** "

I had to Obey The Voice.

I knew that at the bottom of the stairwell, I would find my twin sister Myrna, hiding from me. Curled up in a little O, her back to me. Just like Old Times in the Womb.

I entered the stairwell at the top. The lights were out. The air was thick. The stairs were steep. And I heard her soft breathing, trying not to breathe.

She could hear me breathe.

Her soft throat, trying not to swallow.

She could taste my saliva.

Her heart, trying not to beat.

She could hear my heart thunder.

She knew I was there.

And I said: **"I'm Coming, Myrna."**

"I'm Coming . . . to Find . . . You . . . "

MUCH ADO ABOUT NOTHING

William Shakespeare

Beatrice, 20s – 30s

After overhearing a conversation, Beatrice confesses.

BEATRICE. What fire is in mine ears? Can this be true?
    Stand I condemn'd for pride and scorn so much?
    Contempt, farewell, and maiden pride, adieu!
    No glory lives behind the back of such.
    And, Benedick, love on, I will requite thee,
    Taming my wild heart to thy loving hand.
    If thou dost love, my kindness shall incite thee
    To bind our loves up in a holy band;
    For others say thou dost deserve, and I
    Believe it better than reportingly.

OUR LADY OF SLIGO

Sebastian Barry

Mai, 50s
1950, Ireland

Mai fondly remembers her father.

MAI. *(Groggily at first.)* He turned me about in his good hands like a piece of soap, all about us the glimmers of things, plates sunken into the queer travelling waters of the dresser, little lost slips of brass and such, and at the centre, the warm pool of bath-water, and me, so tiny, perfect, true, washing me tiny toe by toe. So I might have been back in Mama's belly again, and no one else alive I ever spoke to remembers such far things, old things. The basin hard as a tooth, white as a tooth, and me a little soiled by daytime doings, so he was washing me. His face nice like a potato, a smile cut into it, the eyes serious like he was reading the *Galway Advertiser*, by the fire, but I was the fire that time, his little fire, his little nest of coals, a fistful of little features, toes, knuckles, eyes closed tight but seeing, and how is that?

OUR LADY OF SLIGO

Sebastian Barry

Mai, 50s
1950, Ireland

Mai relives the birth of her dead son.

MAI. *(Sister gone, Mai puts the old photo to her cheek.)* Out of the secret pains and terrors of his mother my child was born. I remember the moon sitting in the corner of the window when it was over, peaceful and pure, the hospital set up on high ground above the Sligo sea and the sea itself silver from the moon. And I had grappled with those big demons of pain that had tried to wrench the vittles from my stomach and I had glimpsed now and then the heads of the doctor and the nurse poised between my open legs, like ferreters waiting for the rabbit to burst forth. And indeed something like a ferret and its sharp teeth seemed to have been placed into me and it was ripping and tearing and biting as it went, down into the very heart of me. I was thirty-eight years old, and wild to bring my baby out into the air. I knew I could do it because of Joanie, I knew I had the fight in me, if I was to be let go free. And I was shouting out continually in that room of rubber and metal and I was in a different place than those sublime technicians, whispering and making decisions between my legs. I was the sea herself and that strong-faced baby was surfacing, at great speed, rushing up, mighty, to break the surface, and it was hurting me, hurting me. And if it wasn't to end just that minute, just that minute, by God they could shoot me and be done with it, for it was not to be endured. And then he was there, and he was sort of long and squeezed-looking and he cried. Colin we called him. And he was not like Joanie, he had not her bullish little head, but he was sweet-natured like an emperer, and would open and close his hands when I sang him the old lullaby. He would open and close his hands and seem to know me and for all those seven weeks of life I sang contentedly and I never drank a drop.

OUR LADY OF SLIGO

Sebastian Barry

Mai, 50s
1950, Ireland

Mai tells us how she met Jack.

MAI. Lovely. The pride of the university. It was a fine thing to be full of pep and go. And one day in Queenie's house in Galway, I met Jack O'Hara. *(Out of bed with all her old pep.)* He was introduced to me as Carson's cousin, which surprised me. Carson's cousin, says Queenie, sealing my fate. But he wasn't Carson's cousin, to the best of my knowledge, and why he wanted to be the cousin of that old bigot I don't know. But I was glad to go out to Strandhill with him, dancing in his father's hall. His father had a band and an orchestra, that is to say, a band when he was playing for us, and the same little crowd of men were called an orchestra when he played for the nobs at weddings. It was a little corrugated-iron place called the Plaza. Everyone went out there in the twenties, by the little road white in the moonlight, or across the strand in the roaring cars if the tide was out. My Dada didn't approve of Jack at all and I wasn't sure I did myself. His mother was a small little person with a bit of a dark backround. No one knew much about her, seamstress in the madhouse, maybe illegitimate, gossip. I could never quite make her out, except the bareness and blindness of her house and the smell of lamb boiling at the back somewhere always terrified me. Jack and his brothers were awful drinkers and I suppose Dada was horrified that his daughter was getting mixed up with such a crowd, dwarves and drinkers and such.

OUR LADY OF SLIGO

Sebastian Barry

Mai, 50s
1950, Ireland

Mai tells us about her relationship with her father.

MAI. *(Sitting up.)* I pierced up out of my slumbers like a gannet surfacing through the salty power of the river tide, and cried out for my Dada, to wake and come and lift me out into the day, though indeed, it was not day yet. And my Dada would come obediently and full of sleep, his eyes two gashed pencil marks, and tenderly mumbling a polite good morning, my Mai, my little Mai, seem to tear me gently from the dreadful realm of monsters and hags that sleep was. And he as hot as midday daisies in his crumpled nightshirt, his moustaches funnily askew, so you would try to straighten them out into their proper jutting selves. And over his lovely head was spreading a continent of skin, an Australia of it, as line by line the armies of his hair retreated from the roaring years. And I would reach up and kiss that naked country, and he would nest his moustaches between my cheek and neck, and be tender and good, and set me in my prison chair and scorch up rashers for me.

PERFECT PIE

Judith Thompson

Patsy, Any age
Present, Canada

Patsy records a letter to her lost friend.

PATSY. "I will not forget you, you are carved in the palm of my hand." *(Dawn breaks. She presses "Record" on the Tape Recorder.)* Marie? Are you sitting down? Cause if you're not I think you better cause you might just get the dizzies when you find out who I am. Now don't turn me off thinkin' I'm some kinda crazy stranger like one of your fans. Because although I am a fan, I am not crazy I don't think, and I'm not a stranger that is for sure . . . I am . . . it's funny I feel a little shy to say, because I'm sure you know who I am at this point, at least I hope you know: that I am Patsy. *(Pause.)* Willet. Now Patsy McAnn but you would know me as Willet. You know? Of course you do: Big red face, hash brown hair? We hung around together near Marmora, Ontario like Siamese Twins till you left town when you were about fifteen or sixteen? Well Marie I have followed your career of course; and I am proud . . . to have known you, Marie. And, well, the reason that I am gettin' in touch with you after all this time, Marie, this thirty some years is I have been. yearning . . . To . . . behold you, I suppose. Because I'll be honest with you, when I have been having a hard day and I'm very tired and it's the end of the day and I'm makin' supper or doin' the dishes and the room fills with oh orange light and I hear the train, the low whistle at the back of our property and I stare out the window and I see — just the glimpse of it, of the train speeding on to Montreal, the crash . . . does flash out, in my mind; like a sheet; of lightning, and when the flash is over, and all is dark again, I know you did not survive. I know in my heart you did not survive, Marie. So how is it? How is it that I see you there, out there, in the world?

PHAEDRA

Jean Racine

Phaedra, 20s – 30s
Ancient Greece

Phaedra is in flux.

PHAEDRA. He's gone. What news assails my ear? What ill-
   Extinguished fire flares in my bosom still?
   By what a thunderbolt I am undone!
   I'd flown here with one thought, to save his son.
   Escaping from Oenone's arms by force,
   I'd yielded to my torturing remorse.
   How far I might have gone, I cannot guess.
   Guilt might perhaps have driven me to confess.
   Perhaps, had shock not caused my voice to fail,
   I might have blurted out my hideous tale.
   Hippolytus can feel, but not for me!
   Aricia has his love, his loyalty!
   Gods! When he steeled himself against my sighs
   With that forbidding brow, those scornful eyes,
   I thought his heart, which love-darts could not strike,
   Was armed against all womankind alike.
   And yet another's made his pride surrender;
   Another's made his cruel eyes grow tender.
   Perhaps his heart is easy to ensnare.
   It's me, alone of women, he cannot bear!
   Shall I defend a man by whom I'm spurned?

PHAEDRA

Jean Racine

Phaedra 20s – 30s
Ancient Greece

Here, Phaedra asks for help.

PHAEDRA. O you who see to what I have descended,
        Implacable Venus, is your vengeance ended?
        Your shafts have all struck home; your victory's
        Complete; what need for further cruelties?
        If you would prove your pitiless force anew,
        Attack a foe who's more averse to you.
        Hippolytus flouts you; braving your divine
        Wrath, he has never knelt before your shrine.
        His proud ears seem offended by your name.
        Take vengeance, Goddess; our causes are the same.
        Forces him to love . . . Oenone! You've returned
        So soon? He hates me, then; your words were spurned.

THE PHOENICIAN WOMEN
Euripides, Translated by Carl Mueller

Jokasta, Any age
Ancient Greece

Mourning for her loss, Jokasta tells how it began.

JOKASTA. Sun, flaring in your flames, what a harmful ray
        you hurled at Thebes that day when Kadmos quit
        seaswept Phoenicia, and came to this country.
        Here he married Harmonia, child of Kypris. His son
        Polydoros fathered Labdakos, father of Laios.
        Men know me as Menoikeus' child.
        My father called me Jokasta. Laios married me,
        but after a long marriage with no children
        he drove to Delphi, to petition Apollo for
        the children he craved for his house. But the god replied:
        "Lord of horse-rich Thebes, do not fling your seed
        into the furrow, flouting the gods. If you make
        a son you make your own murderer. Your whole line
        will wade through blood." Yet Laios did succumb to lust.
        Flush with liquor, he planted a seed in me.
        Then, seeing his mistake, and recalling the god's words,
        he gave the child to cowherds to discard
        in the meadow of Hera under the scaur
        of Kithairon, first inserted spikes of iron
        through his ankles. Hence the name "Oedipus,"
        "Swell-foot," by which Greece came to know him.
        But the men who minded Polybos' horses
        carried this child to their chief, and laid him in
        their mistress' lap. She received the result of my birth pangs,
        put it to her breast, and persuaded her lord
        she'd borne a boy. Later, when his first beard

had begun to bloom, either having thought things out for himself, or having heard the gossip, my son departed for Delphi to discover his true parents' identity.

PIZZA MAN

Darlene Craviotto

Julie, 20s – 30s
Present, New York

The phone rings, Julie answers it.

JULIE. *(Crosses to it. Into phone.)* Talk quickly, I'm having a nervous break-down. *(Beat.)* Look, Mr. Plotkin, give me a break! It's hot. I've had a bad day. It's Friday night and I don't have a date. And I'm not looking for-ward to spending the evening with my neurotic roommate. Allow me this one hour in my own apartment to go beserk! *(Beat.)* Doing? *(Beat.)* I'm not doing anything. *(Beat.)* I *am not* dancing naked in my apartment! *(Picking up the phone and moving to the window. Shouting at him through it.)* And what the HELL are you doing looking in my window?!!! *(Beat.)* The curtains are closed. They're thin curtains. *(Beat.)* I won't put under-wear on. I have underwear on. *(Beat.)* I do. *(Beat.)* I do. I do, GOD-DAMNIT, I DO!!! *(Her back to the audience, she rips open her workshirt, exposing herself in front of the window. A beat. She looks down and discov-ers to her horror that she is in fact naked.)* Oh my God. *(Picking up the phone quickly.)* I'm sorry, Mr. Plotkin. I could have sworn I had under-wear on. *(Beat.)* Hello? . . . Mr. Plotkin? Hello? . . . Oh God. *(She hangs up quickly. Stands a moment looking totally lost and embarrassed. She hugs the shirt tightly to her body and hurries toward the bedroom to put on some clothes.)*

PIZZA MAN

Darlene Craviotto

Julie, 20s – 30s
Present, New york

Julie tells Mr. Plotkin off.

JULIE. *(Into phone, matter-of-factly.)* Good evening, Mr. Plotkin. It's 7:45 and you're trying to sleep and you want me to turn down my music, right? *(Beat.)* I knew it was you, Mr. Plotkin because for the last two years you have called me every night and asked me to turn down my music. And *every night* for the last years I've turned it down. *(Deep breath. Bravely announcing.)* Tonight . . . I'm not turning it down! *(Beat. She listens politely.)* I understand that. *(Beat.)* I understand you're a senior citizen and you need your sleep. *(Her anger mounting.)* But the fact is, Mr. Plotkin, you're an old fuck . . . *(Correcting herself quickly.)* . . . FART . . . *(what the hell.)* . . . A FUCK FART! *(She slams down the receiver and heads quickly into the kitchen. Suddenly, she stops and thinks a moment; puzzled by her emotional snit with an old man. She mumbles quietly.)* "Fuck fart?" *(Shaking her head, she continues into the kitchen and grabs another beer quickly. Opening it, she takes a long belt and moves back into the living room. Closing her eyes, she lets the music take hold of her. She sways her body sensually to the hard bass beat of the song.)*

PSYCHOPATHIA SEXUALIS

John Patrick Shanley

Lucille, 20s –30s
1990s, New York City

Lucille talks to her parents.

LUCILLE. Sunflowers! Sunflowers, that will be my bouquet! I will not be contradicted! Daddy, he's not a deadbeat, he's an artist! No, that does not mean vagrant. I don't know if he's any good! I don't know about such things. But he is going to be my husband. That's what you have to deal with. What's Mommy say? Well, you listen to her. I'm wearing it now. It's not bad luck for me to see it! What's she saying? Put her on. Mommy, how do you keep him off the furniture? White. It's white. Pure white. Well, what was I gonna do? Put the approximate number of dots on it? I don't know what you'd call the style other than just classic. It's a beautiful dress. Well, I couldn't very well do that, could I? Your dress is forty years old. It's yellow. It's yellow like an old man's teeth is yellow! *(Knocking comes at the door.)* I'm coming, Ellie! *(To phone.)* It's Ellie. I gotta go. YOU take care! Get that old crank to take you to the Crescent Court for lunch! Make him buy you a Bloody Mary. You tell him I said! I'll be back on with you tonight.

RAISED IN CAPTIVITY

Nicky Silver

Hillary, 30s – 40s
Present, New York City

Hillary talks to us about her beliefs.

HILLARY. I had no God. And although, intellectually, I have always found the idea of "God," per se, rather far-fetched and revoltingly patriarchal, and *organized* religion seems, to me, to be little more than another systematic mechanism by which the plutocratic echelon controls the educational and economic underclass, it does also, obviously provide that subclass a system, with which those who feel burdened by sociologically imposed guilt can purge those feelings, and continue their lives in a clean, new, virgin state.

I went to the church near my house and told the priest that I was bad and I wanted to make a confession. I said, "Father, I am bad. I am pocked with the mark of Cain." He asked me when I last made a confession, and I told him never. He said he was unclear as to what, exactly, my sins were. And I told him that I couldn't be any clearer right now, but that my spirit was spent from shouldering a tremendous, nameless guilt. Then he asked me if I wanted to buy a chance in the church raffle. The grand prize was a microwave. I told him no. I wouldn't feel comfortable buying a raffle and supporting an organization that refuses to recognize women as priests. I couldn't contribute because I believe a woman has the right to control her own body. I feel condoms should be distributed in the public schools because of the AIDS plague and I don't think everyone who uses birth control pills goes to hell. He told me to get out and return only after I'd rethought my positions. Apparently, the price of absolution is the sacrifice of one's own moral code. So I left without redemption and it is up to me to create my penance. I wear these rags as a crown of thorns. I hate them. I have plenty of money. My father invested wisely and left me a chain of motor lodges when he died, but I've been wearing the same dress for five months now. I smell miserable, but I still feel guilty. I tried to give up television — I thought that would be sufficiently torturous to leave me feeling clean and reborn. So I threw my set into the river. But I found myself browsing, decadently, for hours, in appliance stores. I am wretchedness itself. That is why I have decided to put my eyes out with this screwdriver. Excuse me. *(She turns her back to the audience and raises the screwdriver high, over her head.)* I WILL BE CLEAN!!! *(As she stabs her eyes, her light goes out.)*

RECKLESS

Craig Lucas

Rachel, 20s – 30s
1980s

Rachel, in her robe and slippers, makes a call for help.

RACHEL. Jeanette? Rachel. Merry Christmas. No, everything's great, but listen, would you and Freddie mind taking a little spin down here to the Arco station at Route 3 and Carl Bluestein Boulevard? No, no, nothing like that, I just came outside . . . Oh, isn't it? It's beautiful, uh-huh, listen, Jeanette, Tom took a . . . Tom . . . It's so ridiculous. He took a contract out on my life . . . A contract? . . . Uh-huh. Right. And, I mean, the man broke in downstairs so I thought I'd better go out of the house, so I climbed out over the garage and I was afraid to ring your bell because you have all those pretty lights and I was afraid he might be following my tracks in the snow — and so I thought maybe you'd just zip down here and we'd have some eggnog or something, what do you say? . . . Jeane — ? No. No, I know, I am, I'm a kidder . . . But — Merry Christmas to you too, Jeanette, please don't . . .

RECKLESS

Craig Lucas

Rachel, 20s – 30s
1980s

Rachel checks in with a friend.

RACHEL. *(On the telephone.)* Jeanette? Yes, Happy New Year, how are you? I'm great. So how was your Christmas, what did you get? . . . What? Oh, right now? Oh, I'm just up at my cousin's, you know. Of course I have a cousin, what do you mean you didn't know I had a cousin? Everybody has cousins. Where? I don't know, Jeanette, right up route — what difference does it make? But . . . No, I'm fine. Jeanette. Do I sound fine? Do I sound fine? Well. Oh shoot, here comes my bus, but listen do me a favor? No, I will, but — I can't Jeanette, but would you look in on the boys for me? When you get a chance? You will? Thanks, but listen, they're closing the doors, I've got to go. Okay. Bye, Jeanette! *(She hangs up.)*

THE RIVALS

Richard Brinsley Sheridan

Mrs. Bulkley, any age
1700s, England

Here we have our prologue.

MRS. BULKLEY.

> Granted our cause, our suit and trial o'er,
> The worthy serjeant need appear no more:
> In pleasing I a different client choose,
> He served the Poet — I would serve the Muse
> Like him, I'll try to merit your applause,
> A female counsel in a female's cause.
>
> Look on this form, * — where humour, quaint and sly,
> Dimples the cheek, and points the beaming eye;
> Where gay invention seems to boast its wiles
> In amorous hint, and half-triumphant smiles;
> While her light masks or covers satire's strokes,
> Or hides the conscious blush her wit provokes.
> Look on her well — does she seem form'd to teach?
> Should you expect to hear this lady preach?
> Is grey experience suited to her youth?
> Do solemn sentiments become that mouth?
> Bid her be grave, those lips should rebel prove
> To every theme that slanders mirth or love.
>
> Yet, thus adorn'd with every graceful art
> To charm the fancy and yet reach the heart —
> Must we displace her? And instead advance
> The goddess of the woeful countenance —
> The sentimental Muse! — Her emblems view,
> The Pilgrim's Progress, and a sprig of rue!

Pointing to the figure of Comedy.

View her — too chaste to look like flesh and blood —
Primly portray'd on emblematic wood!
There, fix'd in usurpation, should she stand,
She'll snatch the dagger from her sister's hand:
And having made her votaries weep a flood,

Good heaven! she'll end her comedies in blood —
Bid Harry Woodward break poor Dunstal's crown!
Imprison Quick, and knock Ned Shuter down;
While sad Barsanti, weeping o'er the scene,
Shall stab herself — or poison Mrs. Green.
    Such dire encroachments to prevent in time,
Demands the critic's voice — the poet's rhyme.
Can our light scenes add strength to holy laws!
Such puny patronage but hurts the cause:
Fair virtue scorns our feeble aid to ask;
And moral truth disdains the trickster's mask
For here their favourite stands,* whose brow severe
And sad, claims youth's respect, and pity's tear;
Who, when oppress'd by foes her worth creates,
Can point a poignard at the guilt she hates.

*Pointing to the figure of Tragedy.

ROMEO AND JULIET
William Shakespeare

Juliet, teenage — 20s

Waiting, Juliet expresses her frustration.

JULIET. The clock struck nine when I did send the nurse;
     In half an hour she promised to return.
     Perchance she cannot meet him. That's not so.
     O, she is lame! Love's heralds should be thoughts,
     Which ten times faster glides than the sun's beams
     Driving back shadows over low'ring hills.
     Therefore do nimble-pinioned doves draw Love,
     And therefore hath the wind-swift Cupid wings.
     Now is the sun upon the highmost hill
     Of this day's journey, and from nine till twelve
     Is three long hours; yet she is not come.
     Had she affections and warm youthful blood,
     She would be as swift in motion as a ball;
     My words would bandy her to my sweet love,
     And his to me.
     But old folks, many feign as they were dead —
     Unwieldy, slow, heavy and pale as lead.

SCENES FROM AMERICAN LIFE

A.R. Gurney

Woman, 40s – 50s

Here, we hear about the fence.

WOMAN. *(Nervously.)* Um. I want to make three quick points about this whole business of the fence. *(Glances at first card.)* Point one. Appearance. I don't like the looks of it. I know we've been having a lot of fires and robberies and terrorism, but I still don't like putting one of those ugly chain fences around the entire neighborhood. Even in the brochure, it looks terribly unattractive. That awful barbed wire. Those ghastly gates. I don't care how much planting or landscaping we do, we are still going to look like a concentration camp. And that's point one. *(Next card.)* Point two. Inconvenient. The whole thing is going to be terribly inconvenient. I hate the idea of having to get out of the car, to put my I.D. card into those gates just so they'll open and I can get home. And what about deliveries? How do the cleaners, and the milkman, and the eggman get in? The brochure simply doesn't say. *(Next card.)* Point three, and then I'll sit down. What about dogs? This fence is electrified, remember. We can train our children to stay away from it, but what about dogs? Or do we have to tie them up? I refuse to do that, frankly. You know our Rosie, our old Lab. It would kill her to be tied up. I won't do it. And yet if Rosie should run up against this fence, she could be electrocuted. So what I suggest we do is, I suggest we call our friends in Shaker Heights, and Concord, and Palo Alto, and all the other places which have put in these fences, and we find out a few more details. I mean, I'm just not sure a fence is the best solution.

SCENES FROM AMERICAN LIFE
A.R. Gurney

Mrs. Bidwell, 40s – 50s

Mrs. Bidwell calls her Psychiatrist.

MRS. BIDWELL. *(Coldly.)* Good morning. This is Mrs. Bidwell . . . Let me speak to Doctor Taubman, please. . . . Yes, I'd say this was important. Not crucial, but important. . . . Thank you. *(Pause; then very brightly.)* Hi! . . . Listen I'm sorry I missed yesterday's appointment. It completely slipped my mind. What with one thing and another. *(Pause.)* No, no. Listen. What I'm calling about is . . . What I want to say is . . . No, Doctor Taubman, I really do think this psychotherapy business is not for me. We're simply not getting anywhere, you and I. You keep wanting me to talk about the most personal things. I can't. No, I just plain can't. It seems so — so whiney. No, I mean it. I'll just have to call on the old willpower to solve the drinking thing. I'll just have to pull myself together, that's all. . . . No, I mean it. . . . No, now send me a bill, please. I assume I don't have to pay for the session I missed. . . . I do? I do have to pay? Now that doesn't seem quite sporty, does it? . . . All right, all right. Just send the bill. Good-bye.

SOPHISTRY

Jonathan Marc Sherman

Robin, 20s
1990s, New England

Robin gives her valedictory speech.

ROBIN. When I was a little girl, I was so *confident* and *certain*, day-dreaming in my suburban Illinois bedroom, all nice and safe and clean and frilly. My parents, who are here right now — wave to the crowd, folks. (*Points.*) That's them. They used to make me settle fights with my play-mates. They'd call them *debates*, but don't let that fool you. They were fights. (*Beat.*) This school's administrators recently paid an enormous sum of money to *settle*. To keep a former professor from taking them to court to challenge a decision *they* made. This doesn't feel like a fight, or a de-bate — not really. This feels like compromise. This feels . . . very *Hol-low.* What is this supposed to mean to us, as we're about to graduate from this place, with diplomas from an institution that tells us to settle? (*Beat.*) I know that eventually, when understanding runs out, there is a need for judgment, but *who* is qualified to judge? And who is qualified to *judge* who is qualified to judge? Who picks the judges? Who decides that it's okay — to settle? (*Beat.*) Everybody in my hometown was shocked when I chose this place, but they shouldn't have been. Martha Graham danced here. I used to envision myself — secretly, of course — as the heir ap-parent to Martha Graham. Here was a *woman* making exotic *shapes* — her shapes made more powerful statements than all the tainted rhetoric in the air. (*Beat.*) If I could only *dance* all of this . . . (*Pause.*) But . . . I can't. (*Beat.*) I've tried to find some truth during my time here, some *wis-dom,* beyond food and sleep and sex and *showers.* What's worth giving to? I don't know. I wish I did. (*Beat.*) I suppose *settling* can also mean coming to some sort of peace, and I do hope we all find some sort of peace in our lives . . . *All* of us. Anybody . . . anybody who's ever been in pain. And whether *we* settle or . . . *not* . . . remains to be seen.

SPLENDOR IN THE GRASS

William Inge

Mrs. Loomis, 40s – 50s
1920, Kansas

Mrs. Loomis gives us the scoop.

MRS. LOOMIS. (*To the audience.*) I suppose you've heard about Bud's sister? (*She waits for a response.*) No? Well that Ginny Stamper is too low for the dogs to bite. She met some man in Chicago (*She leans forward conspiratorially.*) and he put her in the family way. Mrs. Stamper had to go there and get her and take her to a doctor to have one of those awful operations performed. (*She shakes her head in disapproval.*) Wilma Dean tries to pass it off as gossip, but I know better. Every word is true. I was at the D.A.R. this afternoon and heard all about it. Mrs. Whitcomb lives right across the street from the Stampers and knows everything that goes on in their house. Ace is fit to be tied, I can tell you that. (*Sympathetically.*) And Bud such a nice boy, too. There's a lesson to be learned from this. That's what happens to girls who go wild and boy crazy . . . Wild and boy crazy . . .

SPRING'S AWAKENING
Frank Wedekind, Translated by Carl Mueller

Wendla, 14
1800s, Germany

The Bergmann garden in morning sunlight.

WENDLA: Why did you slip from the room? To look for violets. Because mother can see me smiling. Why can't you keep your lips together anymore? I don't know. I really don't know. There are no words.— The path is like a plush carpet. Not a stone. Not a thorn. My feet aren't even touching the ground.— Oh, God, I slept so sweetly last night. This is where they used to be. I feel as solemn as a nun at communion.— Dear little violets.— All right, mother, I'll put on my old sack-dress.— Oh, God, why doesn't someone come that I can throw my arms around his neck and tell him everything!

SPRING'S AWAKENING
Frank Wedekind, Translated by Carl Mueller

Frau Gabor, Age unknown
1800s, Germany

Mrs. Gabor sits and writes.

MRS. GABOR:
Dear Mr. Stiefel,

I write to you with great sadness. I have considered and reconsidered your request for the last twenty-four hours. Believe me when I say that I am unable to provide you with the passage money to America. In the first place, I don't have that much on hand; and in the second, if I did, I couldn't in any good conscience help you to carry out so rash and serious a plan. Please do not see in my refusal any failure in my affection toward you. I am, of course, prepared to write your parents to convince them that you have done everything possible during this school term, and that to punish you for your failure to be promoted would not only be unjust, but a blow to both your mental and physical health. Quite frankly, my dear Mr. Stiefel, I consider your implied threat to take your own life in the event that you are unable to flee to be a momentary loss of judgment which has somewhat alienated my sympathies. Your attempt to make me seem responsible for your possible commission of a grievous sin seems very much like blackmail. Such behavior is the least I should have expected of you. I realize, however, that the shock you have suffered may well have made you unaware of your action.— I hope that by now you find yourself in a better frame of mind. Accept the matter as it stands. I do not believe that it is in any way proper to judge a young man by his school marks. We have too many examples of very bad students becoming remarkable men, and, conversely, of excellent students distinguishing themselves in no particular way whatever. I assure you, however, that your misfortune will in no way be allowed to alter your relationship with Melchior. I will always be pleased to see my son in the company of a young man who — let the world judge him as it may — has won from me my fullest sympathy. And so, my dear Mr. Stiefel, be brave. If we all committed suicide as the solution to our problems, soon there would be no one left in the world. Let me hear from you again soon, and accept these heartfelt greetings from your ever steadfast and motherly friend,

Fanny G.

STANDING ON MY KNEES

John Olive

Catherine, 20s
1980s, Large U.S. city

Catherine hears voices.

CATHERINE. They used to fly at me. (*Beat.*) Like bullets. Like bullets, they'd mushroom inside me, expanding and twisting, growing, always making a bigger hole leaving. (*Pauses, then laughs.*) No, not like that at all, nothing like that. (*Beat.*) Music. Yeah, more like music. Bartok poems, Crumb poems, Coltrane poems, Ives poems, even Beethoven poems when I was young. Younger. (*Beat.*) Always in a woman's voice. (*Beat.*) Percussion poems. Saxophone poems, always about the night. Poem for — (*Tapping on objects on the desk.*) — number two pencil, empty wine bottle, and broken coffee cup. Solo violin poems, about flying. Bach partita poems. Poem for unaccompanied girls chorus. (*Beat.*) Fly at me. White dream-voice-music-bullets, from the darkness.

THE STORM
Alexander Ostrovsky

Katerina, 20s – 30s
1800s, Russia

Katerina lets us in on her pain.

KATERINA. What is she doing? Just exactly what is she up to? She's crazy, she really is. And look at this — this is my destruction! I'll get rid of it, I'll throw it away, I'll fling it in the river where no one'll ever find it. Oh God, it's burning my fingers like a hot coal. Yes, that's how women like us are ruined. You think it's fun, being imprisoned like this? All kinds of ideas come into your mind. And if an opportunity arises, well, some women would be delighted — they'd jump at the chance. But how can they do that, without thinking, without weighing the consequences? One fatal step, that's all it takes. Then you'll spend the rest of your life weeping, torturing yourself. Imprisonment will seem even more bitter. And it *is* bitter, oh God, it's a hard, bitter thing, never to be free! Who wouldn't weep? And no-one weeps more than a woman. Look at me now. I go on living, and suffering, without ever seeing a chink of light. And I never shall, I know that. The longer I live, the worse it'll get. And now I have this sin on my conscience. If it weren't for my mother-in-law! . . . She's crushed my spirit. Because of her I've grown to loathe even her house — the very walls disgust me. *(Looks at the key.)* Get rid of it? Of course, I must get rid of it. How did it come to fall into my hands? To tempt me — to tempt me to my ruin. Oh God, someone's coming. My heart's starting to pound. *(Puts the key in her pocket.)* No. There's no one there. Why was I so frightened? And I've hidden the key. Well, it seems I knew what to do. Obviously, it's what fate itself wants. Anyway, where's the harm in just looking at him, just once, from a distance. Or if I even spoke to him, what's so terrible about that? All right, I did promise my husband . . . but Tisha himself didn't want me to. And maybe I'll never have a chance like this again. Yes, you'll feel sorry for yourself then — you had the chance, and you didn't take it. What am I saying? Why am I trying to deceive myself? I'd gladly die, if I could even just see him. Who am I putting on this act for? Get rid of the key? No, not for anything in the world! It's mine now — and I'll see Boris tonight no matter what happens! Oh, if only the night would come quickly! . . .

TANTALUS II: PRIAM

John Barton

Cassandra, 20s – 30s
Ancient Greece

Cassandra talks to Apollo.

CASSANDRA.
>Do you remember me?
>Cassandra, Priam's daughter.
>All is happening now
>As it happened long ago
>In my mind: is it possible
>That because I foresaw it
>I have somehow made it happen?
>
>I can speak to you now because
>Though you are yet to come
>We share the same knowledge,
>Though only a part of it.
>This is where my parents brought me
>And my brother when we were babies.
>They feasted here all day
>In honour of Apollo;
>By nightfall both were drunk,
>So they reeled back to bed
>And forgot to take us with them.
>In the morning they found us asleep
>And the two sacred serpents
>Were licking our genitals.
>That is how we became prophets:
>Because they forgot us,
>Because they left us out.

When I saw what was to come
I tried to forget it,
So I went to the stream of Lethe
But by mistake I drank
Of the cold stream of Memory.
Ever since I have remembered
All that is going to happen,
But no one believes me.

See how the sacred serpents
Twist and twine together.
Listen to what they're whispering
And mark the words they say:
"The First Things and the then things
And the things that must follow . . . "
It is time for the Horse:
I curse you, Apollo.

TROILUS AND CRESSIDA

William Shakespeare

Cressida, 20s – 30s

Cressida expresses her true feelings about the game of love.

CRESSIDA.
>Words, vows, gifts, tears, and love's full sacrifice
>He offers in another's enterprise;
>But more in Troilus thousandfold I see
>Than in the glass of Pandar's praise may be.
>Yet hold I off. Women are angels, wooing;
>Things won are done; joy's soul lies in the doing.
>That she beloved knows naught that knows not this:
>Men prize the thing ungained more than it is.
>That she was never yet that ever knew
>Love got so sweet as when desire did sue.
>Therefore this maxim out of love I teach:
>"Achievement is command; ungained, beseech."
>Then, though my heart's content firm love doth bear,
>Nothing of that shall from mine eyes appear.

TWELFTH NIGHT

William Shakespeare

Viola, 20s – 30s

Confused, Viola speaks about her situation.

VIOLA. I left no ring with her: what means this lady?
  Fortune forbid my outside have not charm'd her!
  She made good view of me, indeed so much,
  That methought her eyes had lost her tongue,
  For she did speak in starts distractedly.
  She loves me, sure; the cunning of her passion
  Invites me in this churlish messenger.
  None of my lord's ring? Why, he sent her none.
  I am the man: if it be so, as 'tis,
  Poor lady, she were better love a dream.
  Disguise, I see thou art a wickedness,
  Wherein the pregnant enemy does much.
  How easy is it for the proper false
  In women's waxen hearts to set their forms!
  Alas, our frailty is the cause, not we,
  For such we are made of, such we be.
  How will this fadge? My master loves her dearly,
  And I, poor monster, fond as much on him,
  And she, mistaken, seems to dote on me:
  What will become of this? As I am man,
  My state is desperate for my master's love:
  As I am woman (now alas the day!)
  What thriftless sighs shall poor Olivia breathe?
  O time, thou must untangle this, not I,
  It is too hard a knot for me t'untie.

THE TWO GENTLEMEN OF VERONA

William Shakespeare

Julia, 20s – 30s

Angry with Lucetta, Julia has torn up a letter from Proteus.

JULIA. O hateful hands, to tear such loving words;
       Injurious wasps, to feed on such sweet honey,
       And kill the bees that yield it, with your stings!
       I'll kiss each several paper, for amends.
       Look, here is writ 'kind Julia': unkind Julia!
       As in revenge of thy ingratitude,
       I throw thy name against the bruising stones,
       Trampling contemptuously on thy disdain.
       And here is writ 'love-wounded Proteus'.
       Poor wounded name: my bosom, as a bed,
       Shall lodge thee till thy wound be throughly heal'd;
       And thus I search it with a sovereign kiss.
       But twice, or thrice, was 'Proteus' written down:
       Be calm, good wind, blow not a word away,
       Till I have found each letter, in the letter,
       Except mine own name: that some whirlwind bear
       Unto a ragged, fearful, hanging rock,
       And throw it thence into the raging sea.
       Lo, here in one line is his name twice writ:
       'Poor forlorn Proteus', 'passionate Proteus'.
       'To the sweet Julia': that I'll tear away.
       And yet I will not, sith so prettily
       He couples it to his complaining names.
       Thus will I fold them, one upon another:
       Now kiss, embrace, contend, do what you will.

UNCLE VANYA

Anton Chekhov, Translated by Carol Rocamora

Elena, 20s – 30s
1800s, Russia

Alone, Elena tells us the truth.

ELENA. There is nothing worse than when you know someone's secret and are no help. *(Meditating.)* He is not in love with her — that is clear, but why doesn't he marry her? She is not pretty, but for a country doctor, at his age she would be a fine wife. Intelligent, so kind, true. No, it isn't that, not that — *(A pause.)*

I understand this poor girl. She lives in the midst of uninterrupted boredom. Instead of people she has some sort of gray shadows, wandering around her, what they say is trifling, all they know is that they eat and they drink, and they sleep. And then sometimes he comes, not like the others, handsome, interesting, charming, as if in the twilight rises a bright moon. Oh, to give in to the charm of such a man, to forget yourself. It looks as if I were a little carried away myself. Yes, I am bored without him; here I am smiling, when I think of him. Uncle Vanya says that in my veins perhaps flows the blood of a water nymph. "Let yourself go at least once in your life." What then? Perhaps, it must be so. To fly away like a bird, away from you all, from your sleepy faces, from your conversations, to forget that you exist in the world. But I am cowardly, I'm shy. I'll be tortured by my conscience. You see. He comes here every day, I can guess why he is here and I already feel myself guilty. I'm ready to fall on my knees before Sonia and ask her forgiveness, and to cry.

WHAT I DID LAST SUMMER

A.R. Gurney

Bonny, 14
1945, Upstate New York

Bonny talks to us while waiting for a friend.

BONNY. You know where this is? This is the place out on the back road where Charlie and Ted and I used to sell lemonade in the old days. I got a secret note from Charlie, asking me to meet him here, so here I am. (*Looks around.*) I shouldn't even be here. My parents would kill me if they knew. They think he's bad news from the word go. My mother thinks he's worse than Ted, even. So I had to lie to them. I told them I was going over to Janice's to listen to the "Hit Parade." Oh God, I'm lying more and more! Is this what it means to become a woman? And why is it we women are always drawn to such dangerous men? I feel like Juliet, in Shakespeare's play of the same name. Who says this whole thing isn't secretly about me? (*She shivers.*) What a scary place this is, at night. Right around here is where Margie Matthews met that skunk. And here's where the Harvey's dachshund named Pickle was run over by the milkman. If I had any sense, I'd go over to Janice's after all. Anything, but stand around and wait for a crazy boy who's run away from his own home! But I can't let him down. Maybe the Pig Woman isn't feeding him properly. Or maybe she's keeping him in sexual bondage. Whatever that means. I've got to stay. It's my duty as a friend and neighbor.

WHAT I DID LAST SUMMER

A.R. Gurney

Bonny, 14
1945, Upstate New York

Bonny tells us why her summer is so important.

BONNY. All right! It's an hour after lunch! Everybody can go in the water! (*Bonny spreads the towel, as if she were on a beach. She speaks quietly to the audience.*) Some times I think this play is secretly about me. That's what I secretly think. Because, for me, this is a crucial summer. All sorts of important things are beginning to happen. My father's letting me skipper the boat occasionally. And my mother says I can smoke, as long as it's in front of her. And I've got a paid baby-sitting job three times a week. (*She calls out.*) It's not cold, Susie. Just go in slowly. Bit by bit. And it'll feel fine. (*To audience.*) And tonight, one of the most crucial things of all might happen. Tonight we might be riding this roller coaster. It's called The Cyclone, and on a calm night you can hear it roar, even though the amusement park is over five miles away! Oh it's the scariest thing! It's built right out over the lake, all rickety and shaky, and they say when you climb to the top, you can see all the way to town. And when you start down, it's so basically terrifying that *women* have thrown their *babies* over the *side!* It costs five tickets per person per ride, and there's a big sign right at the gate saying you have to be at least sixteen before you can ride it. But Ted knows the Canadian boys who take tickets, and right now he's seeing if they can sneak us on. (*Calls out.*) Nobody goes out beyond the sandbar, please! Stay in the shallow water where I can see you!

THE WISDOM OF EVE

Mary Orr

Karen, 30s – 40s
1960s, New York City

Karen tells us about Eve.

KAREN. I'm happy to say that all went well. Eve stayed as silent as a
mouse as far as I was concerned. And Lloyd had a great time directing
his own play. He said Eve was the hardest working actress he'd ever seen.
She even persuaded him to coach her in the evenings. The play turned
into a smash hit and Eve became Broadway's newest star. Margo even went
back on the opening night with Clement and congratulated her. Privately,
I knew it was Margo's greatest performance. Time passed. The opening
was in October. Now it was June. Eve was leaving the cast. Her agent —
Bert Hinkle's greatest rival — had got her a three-picture deal in Hollywood. She was being replaced by little Vera Franklin, who hadn't had a
job all season.

THE WISDOM OF EVE

Mary Orr

Margo, 30s – 40s
1960s, New York City

Here, Margo gives us the whole story of what's happened to Karen and Eve.

MARGO. *(To the audience.)* Karen started this story with a prologue. In order to save her further embarrassment, I'll give you the epilogue. Karen went to Sun Valley and got her divorce. The judge gave her a million dollars and the country house. All Lloyd got was the family cat. Eve and Lloyd were quickly married. Eve made two pictures on the coast. They were not very good. Just routine. That happens all the time in Hollywood. They buy a Broadway actress because she's unique and then don't know what to do with her. However, I think you will find in the future that her film career is going to pick up. There was a rumor printed in "Tally-Ho's" column last week — and you know what a first-class ferret he is — that all was not well in the Robertses' menage. Eve's constantly seen around town with a top-flight movie mogul. Can it be that love has worn off so soon? Is Lloyd just another stepping-stone in the career of this talented young actress? Only time will tell. *(She points her finger upwards.)* But, believe me, Eve, you'd better stay up there on your starry pedestal. Because once you begin to slip, a lot of people will be eager to kick you on your way down. *(She gets off the stool, picks it up and starts to walk toward the stage door corner. She pauses for a moment.)* Oh — one final word. If any of you have daughters with stage ambitions, take my advice. Tell them — all about Eve. *(She continues on her way and disappears through the stage door.)*

THE WISDOM OF EVE

Mary Orr

Karen, 30s – 40s
1960s, New York City

Karen gives us a brief introduction.

KAREN. Ladies and gentlemen, I'm Mrs. Lloyd Roberts. Before I married I was an actress. My stage name was Karen Anders. I wasn't very successful. Oh, I had talent, but talent is not enough to make you a star. You need other qualities . . . Tonight I'm going to tell you about a girl who *does* have these qualities. Her name is Eve Harrington.

It was nearly two years ago when I spoke to Eve for the first time. She was standing at the stage door of the Circle Theatre waiting for Margo Crane to come out. Margo is not only a tremendous force in the theater, she is my best friend. She has been the star in three of my husband's smash hits. My husband, you will gather, is a playwright . . . Margo is marvelous. A dream, when she's not being a nightmare. Like all stars she is surrounded by satellites. Eve Harrington used to be one of them — an autograph hound, a nobody. When I first saw her she was just a little ghost haunting the shadows of a dark alley . . . *(She gestures toward the right by the footlights.)* Picture over in that corner the stage door of the Circle Theater. It's at the end of a long, dark passage. No one would dare to venture down it but actors, who are never afraid of anything — except dramatic critics. It was one of those misty November evenings when the elements were undecided. To rain or not to rain. So, since a faint drizzle was dampening the alley, Margo's fans had not appeared at the stage door in their usual numbers. In fact, there was only one. Eve Harrington! . . .

WIT

Margaret Edson

Viv, 40s – 50s
1990s

Viv tells us what it's really like.

VIVIAN. In this dramatic structure you will see the most interesting aspects of my tenure as an inpatient receiving experimental chemotherapy for advanced metastatic ovarian cancer.

But as I am a *scholar* before . . . an impresario, I feel obliged to document what it is like here most of the time, between the dramatic climaxes. Between the spectacles.

In truth, it is like this: *(She ceremoniously lies back and stares at the ceiling.)*

You cannot imagine how time . . . can be . . . so still.

It hangs. It weighs. And yet there is so little of it.

It goes so slowly, and yet it is so scarce. *(Pause.)*

If I were writing this scene, it would last a full fifteen minutes. I would lie here, and you would sit there. *(She looks at the audience, daring them.)*

Not to worry. Brevity is the soul of wit.

But if you think eight months of cancer treatment is tedious for the *audience*, consider how it feels to play my part.

All right. All right. It is Friday morning: Grand Rounds. *(Loudly, giving a cue.)* Action.

THE WOOLGATHERER

William Mastrosimone

Rose, 20s – 30s
1970s, South Philadelphia

Rose is talking to an imaginary Cliff.

ROSE. Shhh! The old lady! Hear her move the glass? (*Pause.*) You have cold feet. You should cut your toenails. (*Pause.*) If your truck ever crashes through a guardrail off a mountain, and you get all crippled up in a wheelchair, don't worry. Everything will still be the same. (*Pause.*) And I don't cheat. Shh! Hear her move the glass? She's hard-of-hearing until you whisper. And then she hears the flowers growing on the wallpaper. Around Christmas she goes a little berzerk. Screams at her son for not visiting her. Throws things. Pots and dishes. But he's not there. Nobody's there. And then it gets real quiet, and if you listen close, like with a glass, you can hear her whimper, like a hurt animal. (*Pause.*) You should rub your hands with cold creme to make 'em soft. You scratch me. (*Pause.*) When you was asleep, I dreamed we were in your truck, riding up this mountain, you know, cross country. (*Pause.*) If you don't mean something, don't tell me, alright? Because it makes me dream, and one dream makes another, and I'm lost in the bigness of the mountain and the curve of the road, and the engine was chugging hard, and there was this thin guardrail this far away and the breeze carried the scent of grass and wild flowers and I got ascared because we got higher and higher and held tight to the seat and you laughed and said, "What's that funny noise?" and I said, "What noise?" and you said, "Oh no! the truck's gonna explode!" and I punched you and we laughed and this cool breeze, this different breeze touched us, this salt breeze, and we came around the bend in the mountain road and all of a sudden this tremendous bright light hit us, and it was so big you couldn't see the beginning or the end and it was the Pacific Ocean glimmering like tin foil rolled out forever, and we couldn't speak for a long time, and way down below us we saw the cities along the coast, like beads on a necklace, and we went down the mountain. And at the bottom we got out the truck and you took my arm and pulled me across the sand and into the waves and I screamed at the touch of the water and you laughed and we both went under and tasted the salt of the ocean and it was so good and we came up and kissed me hard on the mouth and I tasted your salt and a wave came over our heads and dunked us under and we laughed and got water in our mouths and spit it at each other and everybody on the beach thought we was crazy but we didn't care because we felt new again.

PERMISSIONS

AGNES OF GOD Copyright 1979 by John Pielmeier. Reprinted by Permission of the Author. Contact: Courage Productions, 39 Foxglove Lane, Garrison NY 10524.

ANDROMACHE Copyright 1982 by Jeane Racine. Reprinted by Permission of Peter Franklin. Contact: Dramatists Play Service, 440 Park Avenue South, New York, NY 10016.

ANNE OF THE THOUSAND DAYS Copyright 1948 by Maxwell Anderson. Reprinted by Permission of Anderson House Publishers and Donald M. Anderson, Dir. Contact: Robert A. Freedman Dramatic Agency, Inc. 1501 Broadway, Suite 2310, New York, NY 10036.

AS BEES IN HONEY DROWN Copyright 1998 by Douglas Carter Beane. Reprinted by Permission of Helen Merrill Ltd. on behalf of the Author. The stage performance rights in AS BEES IN HONEY DROWN (other than first class rights) are controlled exclusively by Dramatists Play Service, 440 Park Avenue South, New York, NY 10016. No professional or non-professional performance of the Play (excluding first class professional performance) may be given without obtaining in advance the written permission of Dramatists Play Service, and paying the requisite fee. Inquiries concerning all other rights should be addressed to Helen Merrill Ltd., 295 Lafayette Street, Suite 915, New York, NY 10012-2700.

THE BEAUTY QUEEN OF LEENANE Copyright 1996 and 1999 by Martin McDonagh. Reprinted by Permission of Dramatists Play Service, Inc. CAUTION: The excerpt from THE BEAUTY QUEEN OF LEENANE included in this volume is reprinted by permission of Dramatists Play Service, Inc. The English language stock and amateur stage performance rights in this Play are controlled exclusively by Dramatists Play Service, 440 Park Avenue South, New York, NY 10016. No professional or nonprofessional performance of the Play may be given without obtaining, in advance, the written permission of Dramatists Play Service, Inc., and paying the requisite fee. Inquiries concerning all other rights should be addressed to The Rod Hall Agency Ltd., 7 Goodge Place, London W1P 1FL, England.

BLUES FOR MISTER CHARLIE Copyright 1964, 1992 by James Baldwin. Reprinted by Permission of the James Baldwin Estate. Contact: Eileen Ahearn, James Baldwin Estate, 137 W. 71st Street, New York, NY 10023, fax (212) 873-5089.

CATHOLIC SCHOOL GIRLS Copyright 2003 by Casey Kurtti. Reprinted by Permission of the Author. Contact: Ellen Hyman Jones, 44 Parker Drive, Pittsford NY 14534.

COLLECTED STORIES Copyright 2003 by Donald Margulies. Reprinted by Permission of Theatre Communications Group. Contact: Theatre Communications Group, 520 8th Ave., 24th Floor, New York, NY 10018-4156, Attn: Terry Nemeth.

COYOTE ON A FENCE Copyright 2000 by Bruce Graham. Reprinted by Permission of Mary Harden a/a/f the Author. CAUTION: Professionals and amateurs are hereby warned that performance of COYOTE ON A FENCE is subject to a royalty. It is fully pro-

GOOD NIGHT DESDEMONA (GOOD MORNING JULIET) Copyright 1990 by Ann-Marie MacDonald. Reprinted by Permission of Grove/Atlantic, Inc. Contact: Susan Schulman Literary Agency, 454 W. 44th Street, New York, NY 10036. Please contact Random House Canada for other rights.

HOW I LEARNED TO DRIVE Copyright 1997, 1998 by Paula Vogel. Reprinted by Permission of Theatre Communications Group. Contact: Theatre Communications Group, 520 8th Ave., 24th Floor, New York, NY 10018-4156, attn: Ben Sampson.

INDEPENDENCE Copyright 1985 by Lee Blessing. Reprinted by Permission of Lee Blessing. Contact: Judy Boals, Inc. 208 W. 30th St., #401, New York, NY 10001

INVITATION TO THE MARCH Copyright 1961 by Arthur Laurents. Reprinted by Permission of the William Morris Agency. Contact: Dramatists Play Service, 440 Park Avenue South, New York, NY 10016.

JENNY KEEPS TALKING Copyright 1995 by Richard Greenberg. Reprinted by Permission of William Morris Agency, Inc. on behalf of the Author. CAUTION: Professionals and amateurs are hereby warned that "JENNY KEEPS TALKING" is subject to a royalty. It is fully protected under the copyright laws of the United States of America, and of all countries covered by the International Copyright Union (including the Dominion of Canada and the rest of the British Commonwealth), and of all countries covered by the Pan-American Copyright Convention and the Universal Copyright Convention, the Berne Convention and of all countries with which the United States has reciprocal copyright relations. All rights, including professional/ amateur stage rights, motion picture, recitation, lecturing, public reading, radio broadcasting, television, video or sound recording and all other forms of mechanical or electronic reproduction, such as CD-ROM, CD-I, information storage and retrieval systems and photocopying, and the rights of translation into foreign languages, are strictly reserved. Particular emphasis is placed upon the matter of readings, permission for which must be secured from the Author's agent in writing. Inquiries concerning rights should be addressed to William Morris Agency, Inc. 1325 Avenue of the Americas, New York, NY 10019, Attn: Steve Spiegel.

JOAN OF LORRAINE Copyright 1946 by Maxwell Anderson. Reprinted by Permission of Anderson House Publishers and Donald M. Anderson, Dir. Contact: Robert A. Freedman Dramatic Agency, Inc. 1501 Broadway, Suite 2310, New York, NY 10036.

LAKE HOLLYWOOD Copyright 2003 by John Guare. Reprinted by Permission of Dramatists Play Service, Inc. Contact: Dramatists Play Service, 440 Park Avenue South, New York, NY 10016.

LAUGHING WILD Copyright 1996 by Christopher Durang. Reprinted by Permission of Helen Merrill Ltd. on behalf of the Author. Contact: Helen Merrill Ltd. a/a/f Christopher Durang, 295 Lafayette Street, Ste. 915, New York, NY 10012-2700.

LUCIA MAD Copyright 1993 by Don Nigro. Reprinted by Permission of Samuel French, Inc. Contact: Samuel French, Inc. 45 West 25th Street, New York, NY 10010.

THE MAIDS Copyright 1954 by Jean Genet, translated by Bernard Frechtman. Reprinted by Permission of Grove/Atlantic, Inc. Contact: Rosic Colin Ltd., 1 Clareville Grove Mews, London SW7 5AH, England.

THE MARRIAGE OF BETTE AND BOO Copyright 1985 by Christopher Durang. Reprinted by Permission of Helen Merrill Ltd. on behalf of the Author. Contact: Helen Merrill Ltd. a/a/f Christopher Durang, 295 Lafayette Street, Ste. 915, New York, NY 10012-2700.

MASTER CLASS Copyright 2001 by Terrence McNally. Reprinted by Permission of the Author. Contact: Terence McNally 29 East 9th Street, Apt. 15, New York, NY 10003.

MEDEA Copyright 2003 translated by Carl Mueller. Reprinted by Permission of the translator. Contact: Smith and Kraus Publishers, P.O Box 127, Lyme, NH 03768

THE MEMORY OF WATER Copyright 1997 by Shelagh Stephenson. Reprinted by Permission of Peter Hagan. Contact: Peter Hagan, The Gersh Agency, 41 Madison Avenue, 33rd Floor, New York, NY 10010.

MIDDLE OF THE NIGHT Copyright 1957 by Paddy Chayefsky, Renewed 1985 by Susan Chayefsky and Dan Chayefsky. Reprinted by Permission of Applause Theatre and Cinema Books. Contact: Regarding publication rights: Rights Department, Applause Books, 151 West 46th Street, New York, NY 10036; regarding amateur theatrical rights: Samuel French, Inc. 45 West 25th Street, New York, NY 10010; regarding professional theatrical rights: Sidney Feinberg, Lazarus, and Harris, 561 Seventh Ave., New York, NY 10018.

THE MINEOLA TWINS Copyright 1995, 1996, 1997, 1998 by Paula Vogel. Reprinted by Permission of Theatre Communications Group. Contact: Theatre Communications Group, 520 8th Ave., 24th Floor, New York, NY 10018-4156.

OUR LADY OF SLIGO Copyright 1999 by Sebastian Barry. Reprinted by Permission of Dramatists Play Service, Inc. CAUTION: The excerpt from OUR LADY OF SLIGO included in this volume is reprinted by permission of Dramatists Play Service, Inc. The English language stock and amateur stage performance rights in this Play are controlled exclusively by Dramatists Play Service, 440 Park Avenue South, New York, NY 10016. No professional or nonprofessional performance of the Play may be given without obtaining, in advance, the written permission of Dramatists Play Service, Inc., and paying the requisite fee. Inquiries concerning all other rights should be addressed to The Agency (London) Ltd., 24 Pottery Lane, Holland Park, London W11 4LZ, England.

PERFECT PIE Copyright 2003 by Judith Thompson. Reprinted by Permission of Playwrights Canada Press and Judith Thompson. Contact: Angela Rebeiro, Playwrights Canada Press, 54 Wolseley Street, 2nd Floor, Toronto, Ontario, Canada M5T 1A5. Fax 416.703.0059.

PHAEDRA Copyright 1984 and 1986 by Jean Racine. Reprinted by Permission of Peter Franklin. Contact: Dramatists Play Service, 440 Park Avenue South, New York, NY 10016.

THE PHOENICIAN WOMEN Copyright 2003 translated by Carl Mueller. Reprinted by Permission of the translator. Contact: Smith and Kraus Publishers, P.O Box 127, Lyme, NH 03768